D1617028

The Comparative Understanding of Intergroup Relations

The Comparative Understanding of Intergroup Realtions

A Worldwide Analysis

Graham C. Kinloch

Westview Press
A Member of the Perseus Books Group

Copyright © 1999 by Westview Press, A Member of the Perseus Books Group

Published in 1999 in the United States of America by Westview Press, 5500 Central Avenue, Boulder, Colorado 80301-2877, and in the United Kingdom by Westview Press, 12 Hid's Copse Road, Cumnor Hill, Oxford OX2 9JJ

Library of Congress Cataloging-in-Publication Data
Kinloch, Graham Charles.
  The comparative understanding of intergroup relations : a
worldwide analysis / Graham C. Kinloch.
     p. cm.
  Includes bibliographical references and index.
  ISBN 0-8133-9025-7
  1. Intergroup relations.   2. Social psychology.   I. Title.
HM131.K495   1999
302.3'4—dc21   99-11950
                                                                    CIP

The paper used in this publication meets the requirements of the American National Standard for Permanence of Paper for Printed Library Materials Z39.48-1984.

10   9   8   7   6   5   4   3   2   1

To a More Peaceful World

Contents

Part Four
Conclusions

Preface

The present work emerged out of my biographical experiences. I was born and spent my formative years in what was then Rhodesia, a typical *colony*, ruled by a tiny white elite who subjected the black majority to rigid racial segregation, exclusion, and control. I attended a high school reserved for white males where I experienced a typically British-type education with major examinations flown in from England. Education in such an environment, while thorough, was authoritarian, rigid, and largely based on rote-learning. This caste-based society appeared orderly and natural to those who most benefitted from it, with many whites fiercely resisting racial change as a result.

In 1960, my family moved to New Zealand where I completed my undergraduate training in a setting where whites were in the majority, but nevertheless failed to treat the indigenous population with much dignity. While this setting lacked extremes in terms of wealth and poverty, its general atmosphere was largely isolationist, static, and introverted. I became very critical of a country which appeared highly mediocre regarding political and economic efficiency.

I returned to Rhodesia immediately upon graduation in 1964, where I taught in a black high school and observed the beginnings of civil war. In response, the white elite resisted indigenous claims to independence and majority rule.

I began graduate school in the United States in 1965, completing my degrees in 1968. This society was experiencing the dynamics of student unrest, civil rights, and protests against the Vietnam War. I returned to Southern Africa for a short period, becoming gradually aware of the rising racial conflict around me. While sensitive to the negative effects of the most glaring kinds of white racism and discrimination, most whites largely continued to ignore the need for fundamental societal change to any significant degree.

In 1970, I moved to Honolulu where I taught race relations at the University of Hawaii. Moving from racist Southern Africa to a setting in which non-racist behavior was the overt norm made a profound impression on me: clearly, racism was entirely socially-created, the invention of particular societal contexts designed to legitimize the major kinds of inequality within them. While racism was not entirely absent in the Hawaiian situation, high levels of interracial tolerance and mixing were striking features of the social landscape. Overt expression of prejudice was neither encouraged nor accepted. I became fascinated by interracial attitudes, stereotyping, social distance, and the interpersonal dynamics of racially-mixed families as these phenomena related to the society's socioeconomic hierarchy. The contrast with the Southern African situation was overwhelming. I became increasingly interested in comparative group relations, culminating in my book, *The Dynamics of Race Relations, A Sociological Analysis* (1974), in which I developed a general colonial theory of race relations applied to individual, group, and societal levels of analysis. This was further elaborated in *The Sociology of Minority Group Relations* (1979), in which this approach was related to a broad range of minorities, including the physically, culturally, economically, and behaviorally-defined. My continuing interest in the Rhodesian situation also resulted in the publication of *Racial Conflict in Rhodesia: A Socio-Historical Study* (1978) which focused on changing white and African racial attitudes in this particular colonial society from the 1890's through the 1970's, based on a broad range of attitudinal and demographic data. This project made me particularly aware of the historical, cultural, national, demographic, occupational, and economic factors behind the dynamics of intergroup relations in this particular country.

Living in Florida, part of the American South, since 1971, I have also experienced colonial race relations in this setting for an extended period, struck by its similarities and limited differences relative to my previous experiences. The United States, while founded on the myth that it represents a liberal democracy, is a colonial situation, nevertheless, containing a fairly rigid racial hierarchy exploited by its W.A.S.P. elite. In this situation, I have continued to research changing race relations, the dynamic situation in Zimbabwe, and, more recently, intergroup conflict on a world-wide basis.

The present monograph represents an extension and elaboration of my earlier interest in the colonial process and its impact on the world as a whole. While my previous work focused on *general* models of colonialism and *particular* situations, this project sought to expand its scope to all major societies around the world and the United States in particular. The result is a study which focuses on the formative historical and ensuing circumstances behind major types of intergroup contact and consequent intergroup relations within approximately 170 countries and all states within the U.S., comparing the more conflict-prone to the more harmonious with respect to a broad range of related factors. My aim was to explicate some of the major factors behind intergroup relations as a whole relevant to contemporary social policies which attempt to address such matters. The approach of such a study is general and comparative rather than microscopic, detailed, and case-oriented. I am *highly aware* of the *limitations* of such an approach: the typologies which emerge are crude, lacking in detail, and are neither exhaustive nor exclusive. Clearly, any particular society or state might fit into a number or none of the categories so developed, while the general conclusions drawn from them may occasionally appear very limited. Obviously, the U.S. and international case studies could be elaborated in a great deal more detail. Nevertheless, given time and space constraints, the 'exercise' reported in the chapters to follow appears useful to the extent it highlights a number of apparently crucial factors behind intergroup violence or relative harmony, raising associated policy implications for attempts at social amelioration either nationally or on a global scale. Particularly interesting, perhaps, is the general conclusion that intergroup contact conditions may override societal contexts, highlighting the possibility of effecting positive social change in even highly problematic types of settings.

In conclusion, I would like to thank a number of people who have helped and encouraged me in this enterprise:

- Jill Rothenberg, formerly of Westview Press, for her enthusiasm and help in clarifying this project;

- Lisa Wigutoff of Westview Press, for her continuous assistance, patience, and advice;
- Adina Popescu, formerly of Westview Press, for her encouragement and help;
- Andrew Berry of Letra Libre, for his patience and exacting work in producing the final camera-ready copy;
- Charles Tilly, Scott McNall, Robin Williams, and Donald Horowitz for their useful reactions to my proposal for this monograph; and,
- Raj P. Mohan, Editor, *International Journal of Contemporary Sociology*, for permission to use my previously published paper, "The Comparative Analysis of Intergroup Relations: An Exploration," *International Journal of Contemporary Sociology*, 30, 1993:173–184, as the basis of chapter 4 of this work.

I am very grateful to them all and greatly hope this small study might contribute constructively to positive social change, if only in a modest fashion.

Graham C. Kinloch

The Comparative Understanding
of Intergroup Relations

PART ONE

Introduction

1

The Importance of
Intergroup Relations

As the world moves toward the twenty-first century, striking types of social antagonism and violence, often genocidal in proportion, persist. Despite significant worldwide economic and technological development, as well as the intervention of international bodies such as the United Nations, situations such as those in Bosnia, Burundi, Haiti, Rwanda, Iraq, Iran, the Congo, and the former Soviet Union display troubling levels of intergroup hatred, violence, and destruction, challenging any optimistic notions of modern progress. Continuing massacres in Kosovo further illustrate the urgent need to deal with the destructive consequences of ethnic conflict, despite its complex nature, particularly in the international context. Recent bombings in the United States, including those at the Oklahoma City Federal Building, abortion clinics, and the Olympic Games, indicate the potential for serious violence in western democracies as well, highlighting the need to understand "cultures of violence" in greater depth. The recently negotiated peace in Northern Ireland has likewise revealed its fragility, as evident in continuing bombing incidents. Finally, violence at *every* level of society, interpersonal, family, group, and international has recently increased markedly in visibility. Regardless of global patterns of economic development, democratization, and third party negotiation, high levels of destructive hostility continue to flourish, apparently unabated.

Why is this the case, despite significant progress effected in many sectors of the twentieth-century world? Why, despite large-scale efforts by international organizations such as the U.N., I.M.F., U.N.I.C.E.F., and others to ensure peace, economic development, and educational advancements on a global scale, do intergroup massacres, sometimes in genocidal proportions, continue to occur all over the world, often unpredicted? Distressing events like these appear to highlight factors inherent within situations which may result in the emergence of intergroup conflict and violence, particularly the historical circumstances under which societies have been founded and the dynamics of their ongoing contact situations. According to this view, societies may be viewed as types of social structures, or combinations of particular contact situations, in which certain kinds of intergroup relations, positive or negative, may be *situationally triggered.* These dynamics are not predictable in any uniform manner: situations viewed as traditionally orderly may suddenly turn violent, reflecting imposed rather than consensual order (e.g., some areas of the former Soviet Union) while societies depicted as potentially conflict-ridden may turn out to be fairly peaceful, at least temporarily—recently independent South Africa comes to mind, a country which, despite its oppressive past and somewhat unstable current situation, remains relatively calm in a fairly unstable region of the world. Most societies obviously fall somewhere between these extremes, capable of provoking relative conflict or harmony. What makes the key difference in any of them with respect to potential social violence? The place to look, this book will argue, lies in the kinds of societal contexts in which intergroup relations take place, particularly their types of *historical* development. Accordingly, these kinds of relations represent major indices of such environments and their evolution over time. Their social significance, consequently, cannot be overestimated.

The Social Significance of Intergroup Relations

These processes are inherently *social,* occurring in the group context: intergroup relations may be defined as the kind of interaction which occurs at individual, group, institutional, and societal levels, using group-based categories or *definitions* of particular *contact* situations. These clearly operate at the individual level through our social selves, identities, and "sense of group position" in relation to the other out-groups around us (cf. Blumer 1958), i.e., our personal identities reflect our position in the larger society, particularly its socioeconomic order. No matter how unique we may think we are, our personal identities are based on and reflect group-defined criteria. They are also very much part of intergroup competition, power relations, and the formation of social movements, as well as race and ethnic relations, class struggles, union mobilization, and the dynamics of inequality generally. Accordingly, group dynamics reflect the nature of a society's power arrangements in action, particularly its system of stratification. As also indicated, societies involve the formation of particular types of social arrangements with relatively unique historical sequences of certain contact situations, both negative and positive, constructive and potentially violent. Consequently, they comprise fairly consistent contexts which either tend to favor or inhibit destructive intergroup behavior. Finally, at the international level, U.N. politics, regional 'theaters,' and recent worldwide responses to genocidal conflict in particular areas, often involving peace-keeping activities, all reflect intergroup relations at work on a global scale. Responses to violent situations in Somalia, Haiti, Rwanda, Bosnia, and Iraq readily come to mind in this regard. From the above, it is clear that intergroup relations are part of our daily personal lives, group interaction, political views and activities, and reflect society's major types of inequality and power arrangements.

These phenomena are a central ingredient of *social* relations at every level of society and beyond, providing important insight into every level of society and related issues. Accordingly, intergroup relations are extremely insightful cues into a society's past development, cultural values, the personal attitudes and identities of its members, predominant types of social organization as reflected in its institutional arrangements, most visible social problems, and political dynamics. In short, these important phenomena highlight any society's formation, present social structure, culture, and dominant social issues. Like a litmus test, they reveal current attitudes, social groups, types of inequality and power, and the general nature of social organization generally. Understanding their development and consequences becomes crucial to dealing with modern social issues effectively.

Analytical Complexity

Attempting to understand them, however, is far from easy. Personal blindness is not limited to ethnocentrism but extends to insensitivity to the complexity of group boundaries and situation-ally-defined identities. It is easy to be simplistic, uni-dimensional, and reductionistic about such matters. The dynamics of these relations are also complex and often hidden, remaining unpredictable and surprising in their outcomes. Furthermore, developing methods adequate to their analysis is extremely difficult, given their complexity and dynamic nature. When trying to understand a large number of societies simultaneously, it is difficult to avoid becoming lost either in macroscopic scope or microscopic detail. Keeping one's clarity of focus is not easy at any point of the analysis. As a result, many typologies tend to be unidimensional and simplistic, based on bifurcations of societal types, while much data is cross-sectional rather than longitudinal, aggravating the risk of drawing inaccurate and distorted conclusions. Analyzing such phenomena in largely demographic terms, furthermore, often produces general and obvious results with little apparent insight into particular societies. Conceptual frameworks often tend to be reductionistic rather than multilevel or multivariate in scope. The difficulties attached to understanding social history also involve ideological and empirical barriers to significant insight, since they tend inevitably to represent the analyst's projected subjectivity to some degree, regardless of attempts at accuracy and objectivity. Examples include the obvious distortions caused by ethnocentrism and nationalism, while the latter reveal the limitations inherent in fashionable conceptual frameworks and methodological techniques, reinforced by the ever-present scramble for scientific and professional prestige, particularly among social scientists. Consequent typological distinctions among complex situations involve inevitable distortions and the drawing of simplistic conclusions. Intergroup relations are obviously complex, dynamic, multilevel, and easily subject to personal, social, and academic distortion. Understanding them fully is a challenging task.

This Project

Regardless of such pitfalls, trying to understand intergroup relations may provide crucial insight into major factors behind violence at *all* levels of society, including the international. Given the pressing need to address conflict effectively in today's world, this topic remains highly important and relevant to contemporary political policies. The author, with his comparative experience in Southern Africa, New Zealand, Hawaii, the American Mid-West and South, combined with previous analyses of minority group relations in a number of societies (cf. Kinloch 1974; 1978; 1979) attempts in this work to delineate some of the major historical, demographic, economic, political, and sociocultural factors behind intergroup relations, both worldwide and within the United States. This analysis concentrates on the primary elements behind types of such relations in all major independent societies throughout the world (approximately 170) and all states within the U.S., seeking to develop a general approach to social organization and draw specific policy implications regarding the kinds of social problems many of these societies experience. Rather than applying general types to specific societies, this study focuses on the reverse, using historical induction as its major methodology. *No* claim is made that such an approach overcomes all the limitations discussed above; rather, we are attempting to take a broad, historical, flexible, comparative approach to intergroup relations in the hope of explicating *some* of the major factors behind their most problematic consequences, particularly destructive violence. This is also *not* an empirically-oriented project in the traditional sense of the term: large-scale data banks are not used to 'demonstrate' that conflict is widespread globally or appears related to a broad range of demographic and other factors; rather, we are concerned with analyzing societies and their predominant patterns of intergroup relations historically in an inductive fashion in order to reach conclusions which may be helpful in addressing pressing policy issues. We are *highly* aware of such an approach's limitations, as will become clear; however, the project's results appear relevant to contemporary political, social, and academic issues, if only in a modest fashion.

Outline

The chapters to follow fall into four major sections: the first is introductory and deals with major types of intergroup relations, the advantages and limitations of the comparative approach, and comparative views of intergroup relations specifically. Part Two examines these relations particularly within the United States, highlighting different types of historical ethnic, racial, and economic contact and their consequences within this society at state and regional levels, highlighting varying degrees and types of colonial foundation. Intergroup relations on a worldwide basis are analyzed in Part Three, concentrating on particular kinds of formative historical circumstances behind these relations, comparing the more conflict-prone with the more harmonious, ranging from the more isolated and traditional, through those subject to external domination, to the most directly exploited. Part Four, the book's conclusions, contains chapters which bring together the above analyses and draws major policy conclusions aimed at reducing social violence and discrimination, maximizing social equality and harmony instead. Here we shall concentrate on the differential effects of varying types of formative historical contact on subsequent conflict or relative harmony, paying particular attention to group levels of independence, and the importance of facilitating minority equality and freedom at all levels of society, including the international. We shall also discuss implications for sociology's role in the forthcoming twenty-first century, professionally, conceptually, and methodologically.

Finally, it is important to highlight the study's clear limitations: for the most part, our approach is *general* and *comparative*, rather than highly specific and case study-oriented (except for the U.S.), in its attempt to delineate *some* of the *major* factors behind intergroup conflict and harmony relating to contemporary social policies which attempt to address these matters. Our focus will be *macroscopic*, in most cases, in the attempt to achieve this kind of comprehension. Consequently, microscopic detail will be absent and any typologies used are considered neither exhaustive or exclusive; rather, they have been developed and applied for the kind of insight they offer into social conflict and related policy implications *generally*. While the author is *highly* aware of their conceptual and empirical limitations, their careful, conscious application appears to provide useful comprehension of these complex matters.

We turn first to outline the major types of intergroup relations we plan to examine.

2

Major Types of
Intergroup Relations

Awareness of and sensitivity to intergroup relations has increased markedly in recent decades, particularly in the wake of greater media attention to this topic in all its varying forms. Researchers have also become more cognizant of their broader underlying factors, including the psychological and social-psychological (see, for example, Billig 1976; Taylor and Moghaddam 1994). Increasing consciousness of conflict on a global scale has contributed to contemporary sensitivity of the crucial importance of this topic generally. This is understandable in light of the frequency with which all kinds of journalists report on and analyze these kinds of events, particularly when they involve spectacular levels of violence.

In addition, some writers feel the field has become defined as the general concept of "human relations" rather than the more restrictive notion of intergroup relations, given its myriad of associated factors and worldwide social relevance (Grambs 1973). Consequently, this topic has general political significance in the modern world on a global scale; nevertheless, it impacts all of us on the individual level as well, as experienced in interpersonal attitudes and social friction. In a sense, we are dealing with the "human condition" when addressing this topic, i.e., the particular *conditions* under which people come together, live and deal with their needs on a daily basis in relation or reference to one another. Clearly, such a topic has tremendous political, economic, and social relevance with respect to *all* major social issues, both in traditional and modern types of society. Whatever the particular issue addressed, whether prejudice, hostility, poverty, education, health, discrimination, employment, or political rights, they all involve varying aspects of intergroup or social relations.

In this chapter we discuss this important subject with respect to the analytical limitations contained in previous approaches, related concepts and factors, major types of intergroup relations, and also formulate a preliminary model of relevant factors.

Analytical Limitations

Various kinds of intergroup relations, while frequently addressed, tend to be analyzed with respect to very limited types of groups, resultant types of interaction, and analytical frameworks. Ethnic and racial groups tend to be focused on most often, ignoring a myriad of others (see, for example Berry 1978), relations are frequently confined to 'majority,' 'minority,' or both (e.g., Yetman 1975), while types of interaction are generally limited to a continuum ranging from the more segregationist to the relatively assimilationist (e.g., Salins 1997). Furthermore, models or typologies of such 'relations' tend to be restricted to reductionistic contrasts between polar opposites. Examples include distinctions between the 'paternalistic' and 'competitive,' (cf. van den Berghe 1976), 'dominant' versus more 'fluid' types of race relations (Mason 1970), those involving high levels of 'conflict' combined with low 'assimilation' and vice versa (Lieberson 1961), major differences between societies involving slavery and those without (Noel 1968), central factors behind 'imperial' and non-imperial types of race relations (Blue 1959), and authors who highlight principal differences between 'colonial-type' societies and others (cf. Blauner 1969; Carmichael and Hamilton 1967; Rex 1970; Cox 1959; Kinloch 1974). Inherent in these general kinds of distinctions is the bifurcation between societies or (regional) situations in which intergroup relations are most negative and/or conflict-prone and the less problematic. While useful as starting analytical guides, these kinds of depictions run the risk of being rather static and simplistic: intergroup relations are obviously dynamic over time and may appear harmonious but contain the hidden potential for violence and vice versa. Apparent surface tranquility should not be interpreted as reflecting a harmonious situation; the investigator needs to dig deeper to locate potential sources of structural inequality and related potential conflict. The basis of these associations may also vary widely with regard to the kinds of criteria involved in social definitions operating at the group level, making their dynamics complex and variable over time.

In this study, we shall take a more dynamic, situational, contextual approach to changing group types in specific historical situations, with corollary varieties of intergroup relations over time. The discussion to follow concentrates on *initial* and *later contexts*, the relevance of *particular contextual factors*, and *resultant types of intergroup relations*. As can be seen, we are particularly concerned with a society's formative background and ongoing settings as they relate to the kinds of intergroup processes which emerge within them.

Concepts and Factors

Intergroup relations are often associated with violence and hostility related to an individual's group memberships (cf. Stephan and Stephan 1996), given the general manner in which in-group solidarity may contribute to antagonism towards out-groups, particularly under threatening and/or other kinds of competitive conditions. Minority group status or diversity is often tied to intergroup tension, hostility, and conflict also (Grambs 1973), reflecting the manner in which ethnocentrism is present in any such situation. Social conflict has been related to an individual's perception of their own social 'categories' or being defined as such by others (Taylor and Moghaddam 1994). Underlying these approaches is the common link between group boundaries, self-imposed or inflicted by others, and consequent intergroup hostility, conflict, or violence, i.e., intergroup conflict tends to reflect and is reinforced by situations of significant degrees and types of power inequalities. Again, then, this topic is a central part of the major issue of stratification and inequality, particularly when conflict is present. Furthermore, the notion of 'social' or 'group' also implies the relevance of such 'relations' at all levels of society—individual, group, and societal. While antagonism may often be expressed by individuals, it reflects the larger societal environment, particularly the kinds of power inequities within it, with high potential for intergroup conflict.

Bringing these approaches together, *intergroup relations* may be defined as the *kind of social behavior, in reference to and oriented by others, which occurs at all levels of society—personal, interpersonal, organizational, and nation-wide.* Personal or individual relations (i.e., types of interaction) involve attitudes such as prejudice and stereotypes regarding the assumed (derogatory or inferior) characteristics (physical, intellectual, emotional, behavioral, and cultural) of other group members, often based on and reflecting significant levels of ethnocentrism and/or other types of prejudice regarding out-group members, involved in everyday interaction with others. Group features include their demographic and ecological characteristics (e.g., group size, types/levels of resources, historical conditions defining intergroup contact), social movements (i.e., group-based reactions and mobilization), group-defined boundaries (e.g., race, class, ethnicity) and the foundation of intergroup interaction, e.g, the economic (i.e., labor), psychological (or ego-based), or normative (i.e., moral or cultural) interests of those in power (i.e., majority elites). Institutional features consist of the manner in which society is organized politically, economically, and socially with particular regard to limited access, unequal resources applied to minorities or those subject to discrimination, and differential organizational goals and related activities. This kind of "institutionalized discrimination" or "organized inequality" is a major feature of general stratification in society at large. International relations operate at the societal level, including the history behind contemporary inter-societal issues and conflict (cf. Kinloch 1979), and intervention of third parties such as the United Nations or regional organizations. Such interactions may be relatively harmonious and equalitarian or highly stratified and conflict-ridden. Finally, these relations are highly dynamic, subject to the ongoing effects of demographic, economic, and political change. The above definition thus views these relations as reflected in personal attitudes, group characteristics, interaction and reactions, institutional arrangements, and international affairs—essentially *all* levels of social organization generally.

Intergroup relations, furthermore, occur in particular *contexts, locations,* and *situations.* The first of these include the effects of economic differentiation, colonialism, and economic specialization, reflecting external influences and potential exploitation (see Kinloch

1979:197; 181–187). Location involves a society's relative isolation and subjection to the influence and/or domination of outsiders. Implicit in all of this is a country's relative independence of such external control or lack thereof. Freedom to live and meet one's needs without the interference and/or dominance of others is particularly crucial to harmonious social relations.

In the first case, societies may (or may not) experience high levels of *economic development* or *differentiation* (e.g., industrialization). This has a major influence on the kinds of inequality or stratification which may emerge within them based on specialized roles, particularly in the form of class, ethnicity, race, and gender. They may also be subject to *colonialism* (i.e., external migration, subordination, and importation of labor groups), further differentiating the society internally ethnically and/or racially. Ongoing industrialization may also result in high levels of *economic specialization* and the kinds of stratification this brings (e.g., age-based and gender discrimination). Some countries have also remained comparatively *isolated* for centuries, relatively unaffected by outsiders for extended periods of time, maintaining their relatively homogeneity and autonomy, while others have experienced continuous external influences from their very establishment. Examples of the former include relatively inaccessible islands and mountain regions while much of the rest of the world has been subject to the latter. Thirdly, some nations have remained relatively *independent* of outside domination for much of their existence, occasionally guaranteed by larger and/or stronger states, while others have experienced high levels of external interference, domination, and control throughout most of their history. Finally, the potential (and actual) consequences of the above factors (in particular combinations) include high (or low) levels of *inequality, conflict and violence*. It is possible to bring these factors together and delineate broad types of intergroup relations.

Major Types of Intergroup Relations

Considering the above dimensions, it is conceivable to distinguish broadly among a number of types of intergroup *situations:* (1) the relatively traditional, economically undeveloped type versus the more modern, developed; (2) the colonial versus non-colonial; (3) the economically specialized or stratified compared with the less specialized; (4) more isolated and less accessible societies contrasted with the highly accessible; and (5) nations with greater or less levels of independence with regard to their levels of political, economic, and social freedom. These contexts, in turn, may be associated with two broad types of intergroup *relations:* (a) those involving high versus low levels of inequality; and (b) the more conflict-ridden compared with the more harmonious.

Bringing together these situational and relational dimensions, it is possible to delineate two very broad types of intergroup relations: (1) traditional, less differentiated, non-colonial, isolated, and independent societies with lower levels of stratification and intergroup conflict, and (2) more modern, economically developed, colonial, stratified, accessible, and dependent countries with higher general degrees of inequality and intergroup violence. While these *types* are clearly general and preliminary, they highlight the vital effects of the following factors on intergroup interaction: migration (colonialism in particular), economic development (specifically differentiation and specialization), ecology (accessibility to external migration and domination) and levels of independence (political and economic). Together, they point to the vital relevance of ecology, migration, economic development, and external relations to understanding intergroup relations within any particular society. These factors, while clearly interactive, may also be divided between the more *internal* (i.e., location and economic development) and *external* (colonial migration and external influences on a group's independence).

Furthermore, social interaction *within* a country may differ significantly in accordance with *regional variations* in these factors, as we shall see: particular areas involve specific combinations of historical and ecological circumstances, migration experiences, types of economic development, and external influences, all of which impact intergroup relations within them. Examples of this kind of diversity include states within the U.S., geographical areas such as Western Europe, and ethnic regions such as Scotland.

Towards a Preliminary Model of Relevant Factors

Bringing the above discussion together, it is possible to delineate a number of factors relevant to the understanding of intergroup relations, both within and external to a particular society as follows: (1) its location or ecology (i.e., remote vs. accessible); (2) migration to and within it (particularly colonial vs. non-colonial); (3) its level of economic development and specialization; and (4) the kind(s) of external relations and influences it is subject to. These factors may be applied to a country as a whole, specific regions within it, and its relations with other nations. Such an approach highlights the kinds of ecological, demographic, economic, and external elements behind the formation of a society as a particular kind of *context* in which social interaction and ongoing dynamics occur at every level. These elements may also be divided into the more *internal* (i.e., location, economic development) and *external* (migration, external relations). Furthermore, the kind of interaction which occurs may be more equalitarian or stratified, more harmonious or conflict-ridden. This model is summarized in Table 2.1, highlighting the manner in which *intergroup relations generally reflect particular combinations of ecological, demographic, economic, and political circumstances under which groups come into contact with one another, societies are formed, and within which ongoing social relations take place.* These factors obviously do not operate in a uniform, consistent manner over time; rather, they are subject to relatively unique combinations of changing circumstances with often unpredictable consequences. Nevertheless, as we shall see, these broad types of societal contexts appear generally related to particular types of intergroup relations within them.

Conclusions

In this chapter we have pointed to the general increase in sensitivity to the importance and relevance of intergroup relations in particular countries and worldwide. In contrast, they have often been analyzed using very limited types of groups, relations and conceptual frameworks. These intergroup dynamics, furthermore, or often identified with violence and conflict at the group level. We broadly defined these 'relations' as involving different kinds of social interaction at every level of society in particular contexts, locations, and situations. Finally, we related a complex of factors or contexts to different levels of inequality and conflict (as varying types of intergroup relations): location or ecology, migration

Table 2.1 Major Factors Involved in Intergroup Relations

Location/Ecology ⟶	*Migration Type* ⟶	*Economic Development* ⟶	*External Relations* ⟶	*Intergroup Relations*
remote vs. accessible	non-colonial vs. colonial	levels of development and specialization	levels of political, social, and economic independence vs. dependence	low vs. high inequality; conflict-ridden vs. harmonious; traditional, less differentiated, non-colonial, isolated, less stratified, more harmonious vs. more modern, economically-developed, colonial, stratified, accessible, more conflict-ridden; effects of internal vs. external factors

processes, economic development, and external influences. Such an approach primarily views intergroup relations in their ecological, demographic, and economic environments.

We turn next to explore the relevance and complexity of the comparative approach to understanding these dynamic phenomena.

3

The Comparative Approach

To state that comparison is part of science is a truism: clearly, examining more than one observation necessarily involves making comparisons of some sort. Furthermore, explanations, macroscopic or otherwise, may be viewed as ultimately based on induction from specific observations to the more general, comparing these empirical instances along the way. However, applying this technique is far from easy: comparisons involve a variety of conceptual, logical, methodological, and empirical complexities. Nevertheless, this kind of approach permits the researcher to explicate underlying factors inherent in an explicit (or implicit) continuum as typologies (or comparative models) are constructed prior to formulating an explicit theory or explanation of the issue at hand.

In this chapter we shall delineate some of the advantages and limitations of the comparative approach, its traditional and contemporary applications in sociology, the kinds of conceptual and methodological issues involved in its use, and why it is so relevant to understanding intergroup relations.

Advantages and Limitations

The advantages offered by comparative research are unmistakable: explication of major factors underlying a continuum along which various cases are examined, prior to development of a more formal explanation or theory. Such an exercise enables the analyst to develop typologies or models highlighting the key characteristics of these instances, potentially resulting in their eventual explanation. Such an *inductive process* is a key part of research and the creation

of relevant conceptual frameworks and possibly more formal theories. Furthermore, comparisons may be made both *within* and
among these cases or types, providing insight into the phenomenon
of interest on a number of analytical levels, thereby elaborating explanations to include both intra and inter-unit variations. This
kind of clarification may also result in significant revision of the
broader theory involved. The addition of further cases only serves
to clarify the researcher's perspective further, offering more detailed and elaborate insight into the underlying continuum being
investigated, resulting possibly in significant elaboration and revision of the basic model.

Such an approach, however, is not without its dangers: comparisons run the risk of becoming simplistic and reductionistic in the
understandable concern to explain everything in unicausal and/or
typological terms. Comparative frameworks may also become *reified*
(or treated as if they were 'real'), taking on an explanatory life of
their own in the context of current academic fads and fashions. Such
'explanations' may also involve oversimplification of the complex,
mask the internal variation of particular cases, and be founded on
spurious interrelationships. A further problem involves the manner
in which comparative perspectives may result in the pre-selection of
empirical cases which fit and therefore 'confirm' the framework, ignoring potentially 'deviant' instances which highlight the need for
more sophisticated investigation.

Despite the above dangers, comparative analysis has played a
significant role in the establishment of sociology and more recent
applications. Provided it is used with conceptual sensitivity and
methodological care, such an approach continues to promise fertile
and very useful insight into modern social problems and issues.

Sociological Applications

Inter-societal comparisons played an important role in sociology's
historical foundation and intellectual development, reflected in
many of the early thinkers' reactions to the perceived effects of industrialization on European feudal society. A number of them, for
example, contrasted traditional and modern, industrial society
with respect to their predominant beliefs, solidarity, motives, and
stages of evolution, highlighting assumed differences between

feudalism and capitalist settings (e.g., Comte, Durkheim, Tonnies, and Spencer). Others differentiated among them with respect to their types of stratification, power, competition, classes, patterns of consumption, and dominant elites (Marx, Park, Veblen, and Pareto are relevant here). Still other thinkers viewed them as differing in their patterns of social interaction, motives, beliefs or types of association (e.g., Weber and Simmel). Implicit in all of these is the distinction between traditional society based on particular types of beliefs, resource structures, and relationships (i.e., the more communal, group-based) and modern industrial settings focused more on individual interests, types of power, and impersonal ties (cf. Kinloch 1977). Underlying this major shift are the societal effects of industrialization effecting greater normative, economic, and social heterogeneity with associated problems of social problems and disunity in the larger society. In a general fashion, sociology was founded in the reaction of enlightenment philosophers to the perceived decline of traditional, integrated feudal society and the consequent search for some kind of natural, scientific basis to social unity in this contemporary, diverse, industrial situation (Kinloch 1977). Implicit in such a reaction was the comparison, no matter how inaccurate, between the past, or traditional types of society, and the emerging modern industrial order. Accordingly, comparative analyses were very much part of sociology's intellectual foundation as these early thinkers reacted to the perceived problems caused by these major kinds of societal change. More generally, comparisons are always involved in a researcher's perception of emerging social problems relative to a past situation assumed to be less problematic.

Implicit in modern sociology is the distinction between orderly and disorderly types of society, evident in the concern by many to maximize structural integration on a behavioral, empirical, or political basis, looking to nature, society, or individual reason as its foundation (cf. Kinloch 1981). In this effort, the major concern with societal *order* is paramount. Others have distinguished societies using types of economic development, location, or systemic position: examples include first, second, and third 'worlds' (Horowitz 1966), north versus south, and position in the "modern world system" (Wallerstein 1974; 1980). Debates have raged over world system/development status distinctions (Weede & Kummer, 1985), world-economy position versus economic development (Rubin-son, 1976; Bollen 1983), the relationship between dependency and income inequality (Nolan 1983), and the relevance of international networks to understanding national economic growth (Snyder & Kick 1979). Implicit in many of these discussions is the distinction between more or less 'developed' and/or 'modern(ized)' types of society with respect to their predominant economic, political, and demographic features (see, for example, Armer & Marsh 1982). While unquestionably different from their earlier counterparts in traditional sociology, a continuing concern with the societal impact of economic development is evident in these analyses.

Both traditional and contemporary sociology, then, indicate a continuing concern with comparative analysis in the continuing reaction of researchers to the radical effects of industrialization on society as a whole. Responding to the evident dynamics of social change, a process which extends at least as far back as the Greeks (see Gouldner 1966), sociologists have always and continue to compare different 'types' of society with regard to their levels and types of 'evolution' or 'development.' In this sense, comparative analysis has always been a major part of sociology in its response to perceived social change, involving contrasts between contemporary and past societal situations. Inherent in these kinds of comparison is a concern with changing intergroup relations, illustrating its potential relevance to this topic.

We turn next to outline some of this perspective's major conceptual and empirical complexities.

Conceptual and Methodological Complexities

Comparative research highlights the conceptual difficulty of distinguishing between specific and general phenomena and interrelating them. Problems include differentiating between systems as a whole and levels within them, the difference between nation states and worldwide systems, clarifying levels of analysis versus observational levels, and major need to define clearly exactly what specific 'objects' are being compared (Ragin 1982). System boundaries also require delineation as well as the distinction between systems and units of analysis (Grimshaw 1973). Attempting such macroscopic explanation requires very clear delineation of systems, subunits, their boundaries, and possible interrelationships when comparisons are being made.

Explicit and clear definition of all sub-elements, their co-relationships at each level, and ties to the macroscopic or systemic level is also required and is a complex task. It should be additionally noted that given the 'multilevel' nature of these phenomena, their relationships may differ at particular levels, regardless of how they may appear when conceptualized as general systems (Nowak 1989). Consequently, it would be erroneous to assume that inter-unit relationships are similar or identical at every level of a social system when comparisons are carried out. Conceptual types and associated comparisons also tend to be overdrawn, reflecting the analyst's desire to maximize perceived differences between units at various points on an underlying continuum.

Once established in the literature, comparative types also tend to become reified, taking on a "life of their own" in consequent research and theorizing activities. While promising, then, comparative research always involves major problems of conceptual definition and logical interrelationship at *every* level of analysis. Accordingly, general comparisons tend to be fraught with possible typological reductionism, simplistic generalizations, and potentially spurious conclusions regarding the presumed relationship between general systems and specific sub-elements within them. Particular care needs to be taken with conceptualization and explanation at each level or stage of comparison.

Methodological complexities include problems of units and levels of analysis, available data, and measurement difficulties. It is clearly challenging to delineate exactly what *units* of analysis are being compared, the difference between observation and interpretation, as well as distinguishing among levels of observation and actual analysis (Ragin 1982). Much data used, furthermore, tends to be non-independent or inter-correlated, key parts of it may be missing, while often very low numbers of societies are relevant to the comparisons being made and are used in their analysis (Ragin 1982). National-level data sources are often very limited, when available, and may reflect government control and/or implicit kinds of censorship in many cases. In addition, demographic data may be cross-sectional rather than time-based, while inflated correlations increase the risk of producing "ecological fallacies" in the results (Taylor and Jodice 1983). Researchers may also find it all but impossible to avoid selecting only those societies which actually *fit* their pre-defined comparative frameworks, thereby inevitably 'confirming' the typological differences they set out to 'discover,' ignoring a range of potential "deviant cases."

Turning to measurement limitations, it is often difficult to know in what ways societies are truly comparable. They are often grouped together in typological contexts when they are not part of the same population, while many, if not all, nations are relatively *unique* in some manner, making such types and comparisons crude distortions of their variety (Ragin 1982). There may also be significant sub-population differences within societies, aggravating the inaccuracy of such group-based distortions, some variables may reflect spurious system-level characteristics, while the key difference between contextual and non-contextual variables may be lost in the anxiety to make comparative distinctions (Nowak 1989). Again, great caution needs to be taken in delineating levels and units of comparative analysis, requisite data and their associated limitations, and distinct measurement problems associated with *any* kind of comparative analysis. While the rewards and kinds of insight provided by such an approach are immense, so are its associated conceptual and methodological problems.

Comparative Intergroup Relations

The comparative approach to intergroup relations permits the analyst to develop an awareness of the major factors defining such dynamics at all levels of society within the setting of society's shift from the more traditional to the modern industrial type. Thus, as nations have been affected by demographic and economic change, the types of groups within them and associated relationships have become more diverse and potentially conflict-ridden. This topic, then, fits well within sociology's traditional concern with the dynamic effects of social change on traditional societies and contemporary interest in the worldwide consequences of economic development.

What emerges is an appreciation of the kinds of societal *contexts* which have developed, both externally and within a country, *within which intergroup dynamics occur and change over* time. In his own work on race and minority relations, for instance, this author has found that macroscopic phenomena such as types of elites, geographical situations, types of intergroup contact, and types of minority are particularly crucial to understanding prejudice and discrimination, while internal variation in such matters appears related to historical circumstances surrounding group contact, and levels of physical, cultural, and demographic similarity to dominant power elites (Kinloch 1974). These kinds of factors tend to operate at varying societal levels and stages of intergroup relations (Kinloch 1979) while, historically speaking, major types of contact situations at the national level appear vital to consequent levels and types of intergroup violence, inequality, domination and discrimination in the wake of economic development and change. Internal relations also differ according to such variations (Kinloch 1993).

From all this, it appears clear that intergroup relations are influenced by a number of major factors over time—historical, ecological, demographic, and economic—as societies worldwide have experienced the complex and differential effects of industrialization, both around and within them. The types of social groups and dynamics emerging within them have varied accordingly. Accordingly, the comparative understanding of intergroup relations fits well within sociology's traditional and contemporary concerns in the context of industrialization and other forms of economic development.

This Project

The project discussed in this work attempts to gain insight into varying types of intergroup relations over time, particularly conflict and violence, by examining all societies worldwide and the United States in particular with respect to their historical development over time. The study focuses on formative historical and ensuing circumstances behind major types of intergroup contact and consequent intergroup relations within approximately 170 independent countries and all U.S. states, comparing the relatively conflict-prone with the more harmonious in reference to a broad range of relevant factors: historical, ecological, demographic, sociocultural, political, and economic. Rather than applying general typologies to specific societies, this study uses historical induction as its major methodology in delineating varying intergroup relations in particular societal contexts. Its major emphasis involves analyzing the relationship between societal context and the dynamics of such relations over time. While clearly restricted to national and regional states, the use of available historical data, a restricted range of relevant factors, and very broad comparisons, our analysis will attempt to provide clear and useful insight into major aspects of this vital contemporary topic.

All states within the U.S. and independent countries worldwide were selected for examination and represent the study's units of analysis. A broad range of historical literature was consulted, as well as more general works (e.g., Kane, Podell, & Anzoven 1993; Wright 1994), to examine each of them. Each U.S. state and country was researched with respect to its historical foundation, key contact frontiers, major political and economic features, demographic pluralism, and levels and types of intergroup violence over time. Units were classified into 'high' or 'low' violence based on the degree to which persistent incidents of violence were present over time in each case. Working inductively, each unit was then sub-classified according to the predominant types of intergroup contact they experienced which were vital to their historical foundation and subsequent development.

The resulting analysis compares intergroup conflict levels within the United States by level of access and colonial contact and those worldwide according to ecological context and type of societal formation, ranging from low colonialism/high independence to the relatively opposite situation. The empirical trends revealed by this are useful in explicating some of the major factors behind societal violence and corollary policy implications. Such an approach is *broad, inductive,* and *interpretive* in contrast to more precise, deductive, and empirical studies. The typologies which emerge from this kind of analysis are broad, lacking in microscopic detail, and are neither exhaustive nor exclusive, requiring further elaboration. Societies were also classified generally into 'high' and 'low' levels of intergroup conflict, rather than using a more detailed, incremental procedure, in order to accentuate societal differences in a manner which dealt effectively with the project's potentially overwhelming complexity. Nor does such an approach pretend to solve the major complications of comparative analysis outlined earlier in this chapter. However, this attempt to take an inductive, dynamic, focused, contextual, and multi-level comparative approach to this subject appears to offer useful insight into apparently key factors behind relative intergroup violence or harmony. Hopefully this will prove relevant to constructive social change, both nationally and on a global scale.

Conclusions

In this chapter we have emphasized that comparison is part of science and any kind of explanation, aiding the investigator in the task of development more formal theories. Use of this approach is also a central part of sociology's foundation and contemporary interests. Such an approach, however, involves some major conceptual difficulties relating to levels of analysis, unit and sub-unit delineation, reification risks, and potentially spurious conclusions. Methodological complexities include difficulties relating to units and levels of empirical analysis, data availability, and measurement difficulties. Despite these kinds of problems, however, we concluded that the comparative analysis of intergroup relations potentially offers important insight into the kinds of societal contexts which have developed over time, within which group dynamics occur and change. We also outlined how we would apply this approach to intergroup relations worldwide and within the U.S., developing a broad, inductive, and interpretive perspective of such phenomena.

The next chapter outlines comparative approaches to intergroup relations specifically, prior to formulating a preliminary conceptual framework as background for the study to follow.

4

Comparative Approaches to Intergroup Relations[1]

Theories are developed by individuals and/or groups of thinkers in response to the kinds of problems and issues most important to themselves. These kinds of *reactions* are neither static nor objective: situations and subsequent reactions change over time while the subjective interests and biases of theorists are reflected in their work. Consequently, theorizing is a highly dynamic and contextual process, neither fixed nor detached from its societal context (Kinloch 1977). In this chapter, we explore the kinds of comparative approaches to intergroup relations, past and contemporary, available to the analyst. We shall also attempt to bring them together in the form of a preliminary synthesis. We begin by discussing approaches to intergroup relations developed by scientists and academics in the past.

Early Comparisons

When applied to the topic of intergroup relations, conceptual approaches to their understanding have been both limited and dynamic over time, shifting from the obviously ethnocentric to the more comparative and relativistic in the context of changing cultural, political, and academic environments. Historically, early definitions of other societies were highly biased and hostile, focusing on the assumed barbarity and inferiority of such "out-groups." Intergroup contacts in such situations were highly likely to be competitive and conflict-ridden, reinforcing the ethnocentric views of all parties involved. These prejudiced views of others, unfortunately, have continued as the basis of many interpersonal, inter-group and inter-societal relations today. Ethnocentric typologies continue unabated in many competitive situations.

Turning to early views of 'race' developed by natural scientists, the idea was introduced into science in early attempts by zoologists to classify the human species into a number of types or sub-types. Banton classifies these thinkers into two groups: those adhering to the "Doctrine of Immutability" and others advocating the "Doctrine of Mutability." The former adhered to a rigid view of race as identified with culture while the latter viewed different groups based on environmental influences (Banton 1967). These relatively rigid taxonomies were significantly reinforced by European colonialism, religious ideas, ethnocentrism, and doctrines such as Social Darwinism. Consequently, these 'scientific' types were reified in a highly stratified international context.

Ironically, racial definitions were largely neglected in the early social sciences, whose advocates conceptualized intergroup relations in social and economic terms instead (MacRae 1960). This neglect of structural inequality was further bolstered by sociology's functional view of American society, generally overlooking its internal inequality (Rose 1968), relatively passive approach to the events of the 1950's and 1960's, emphasis on individualism rather than group dynamics, and a shift towards managing rather than advocating social change in response to government funding and policy needs (Taylor & Moghaddam 1994).

Academic analyses of American race relations reflected largely establishment perspectives, moving from defending slavery, through the assumed inferiority of racial minorities in the context of segregation (Frazier 1947), to attempts to improve race relations using a more social psychological approach (Blumer 1958), efforts to reduce racial tension (Williams 1947), a major concern with prejudiced attitudes and behavior as indices of intergroup conflict (Williams 1947), and eventual shift towards more comparative, empirical, and theoretical approaches to this issue (van den Berghe 1967; Schermerhorn 1970). As racial conflict moved center stage and minority academic perspectives received greater visibility, a more structural, conflict-oriented approach to the topic became apparent. Complicating these limitations was white American culture with its Anglo-Saxon Protestant Ethic values defining all others as different and inferior in *every* respect—physically, intellectually, emotionally, behaviorally, and culturally (Gossett 1963; Kren 1962). Highly racist viewpoints and political policies ensued and were reflected in academia also. Substantive boundaries both among and within disciplines have also made the theoretical task more difficult as psychologists, political scientists, economists, and sociologists have "carved out" and developed their own particular piece of the "intellectual pie" in relative isolation of one another.

Generally, then, theoretical approaches to intergroup relations have proceeded through a number of stages, reflecting a variety of political, academic, and cultural contexts. These began with the openly ethnocentric, moving through scientific taxonomies, intellectual neglect, ideological defenses of inequality, and psychological conceptualizations to the more theoretical, comparative, structural, empirical, and conflict-oriented. Such shifts, however, continue to reflect the cultural biases of the analysts involved, highlighting the restrictions imposed by their own ethnocentrism, regardless of their assumed scientific objectivity, aggravated by professional boundaries. Consequently, despite the apparent movement away from the more openly ethnocentric and attitudinal to the comparative and structural, the need for awareness of the inherent biases and limitations involved in *any* perspective, regardless of how scientific or popular it may be, remains crucial in evaluating any approach to this complex topic.

Comparative Approaches

Approaches to the analysis of intergroup relations may be viewed in at least two ways: as different *types* of theory or as involving particular *explanatory factors.* Some authors, for example, have delineated a number of theories as applicable to particular types of intergroup relations. Banton (1983), for example, reviews ecological, Freudian, Structure-functional, class, pluralist, and split labor market theories of "racial and ethnic relations," applying rational choice theory himself in some detail. Rule (1988) has also evaluated various theories of "civil violence," including the approaches of traditional thinkers such as Hobbes, Marx, Pareto, Durkheim, Weber, and Simmel, as well as "value integration" and "relative deprivation" theories. Others have indicated how differing ver-

sions of the same theory may change over time in response to political events, specifically the primordial and instrumental ver-
sions of modernization theory (Gurr & Harff 1994). Analyses of
race relations have also been divided into the psychological,
social-psychological, and psychological (Kinloch 1974) while a
range of social psychological theories have been applied to intergroup relations on the international level: Freudian, realistic conflict, social identity, equity, and relative deprivation theories included (Taylor & Moghaddam 1994). While useful for heuristic
purposes, such an approach tends to be limiting in the range of
factors applied to the issue at hand. Specification of a broad range
of relevant components outlined in the relevant literature prior to
delineating underlying causes may be a more comprehensive and
useful approach to the problem.

We turn to do so. Review of a broad range of literature, dealing
with a variety of types of intergroup relations, resulted in the delineation of a number of broad factors relevant to their understanding: historical, demographic, ecological, economic, sociocultural, political, and psychological. These involve major societal,
population, situational, labor market, cultural, state, and psychological factors defining particular types of intergroup relations.

Historical Factors

Historical factors involve the specific circumstances under which
groups come into contact with one another in particular societal situations, i.e., the *formation* of particular *types* of societies. In this regard, some years ago Lieberson (1961) developed a "societal theory" of "race and ethnic relations." What is critical, according to
him, is each groups's attempt to maintain and further develop a social order which is compatible with its previous way of life
(1961:903). He proceeds to distinguish between two broad types of
contact situations: those in which a migrant group subordinates an
indigenous population and vice versa (1961:903). The former comprise imposed social arrangements, high levels of intergroup strife,
decline of indigenous populations, low levels of economic assimilation, immigration of outside groups, and significant emergence of
racial unity, nationalism, and conflict. Indigenous control of migrant populations, on the other hand, involves more stable, local

social organization, less intergroup discord, higher levels of economic and social assimilation generally, and more controlled immigration of new minorities. In general, attempts by migrant elites to maintain their lifestyles result in considerably higher levels of intergroup conflict than those produced by indigenous governments.

Migrant elites, additionally, frequently conform to Hartz's notion of 'fragment' societies which broke off from Europe during a revolution which eventually resulted in its modernization (1964:3). Particular situations embody specific stages of this history: 'feudal' in the case of Latin America and French Canada; 'liberal' in the United States, Dutch South Africa, and English Canada; and 'radical' (in the sense of the proletarian conflict involved in the Industrial revolution), typified in Australia and British South Africa (1964:3). Feudal fragments are likely to produce peasant-type minorities, the liberal involve elite racism (1964:34), while radical situations typically result in class-based political movements. Additionally, these kinds of society typically become relatively immobile (1964:3), resisting change as they attempt to maintain their origins in a foreign context. Conservatism and conflict are inevitable, as is the agitation of subordinate minorities in the wake of 'modernity' (1964:44). Fragment societies, given this conservative, immobile, and atrophied reaction to their alien contexts, are generally discordant, with particular historical segments (or "phases of the European revolution") involving definite kinds of intergroup relations (peasant, slave, and labor-based). Each 'fragment's' national origin also results in significant colonial variation: Spanish colonists were feudal and highly profit-oriented, France treated its dependencies in an absolutist fashion, granting them few rights, the Portuguese were imperial and slavery-oriented, as were the Dutch, while the British distinguished between their dominions, granting them relatively high levels of settler self-government) and dependencies which were governed directly and autocratically (Fieldhouse 1967). Moreover, colonies with feudal-type origins (especially the Spanish) were more accepting of their peasant-type minorities while the liberal (particularly the British) continued to be exclusive and segregationist regarding the racial (and often enslaved) groups they subordinated (Hartz 1964). Colonies reflect particular "ways of life" which migrant elites strive to maintain in alien environments.

A number of studies have also highlighted the oppressive be-havior of migrant elites: they are typically disproportionate in size relative to the populations they control (Mason 1970), are highly ethnocentric and competitive in orientation (Noel 1968), and rep-resent capitalistic and imperialistic interests (Blue 1959), often re-sulting in military conquest and frontier expansion (van den Berghe 1967). Intergroup contact in such situations tends to be overwhelmingly negative, involving domination (Banton 1967), and high levels of value conflict (Schermerhorn 1964), leading to gross power imbalances (Bagley 1972; Noel 1968; Schermerhorn 1964) and high levels of racial stratification (Blue 1959; van den Berghe 1967). The minorities they create are often heterogeneous (Mason 1970) and highly exploited for economic gain (Cox 1959).

Generally, societies settled and controlled by external elites may be depicted as 'colonial' in nature, in which a migrant elite con-quers an indigenous population, brings in other racial groups for labor purposes and rationalizes its elite position in racist terms (Kinloch 1974:225). Often initial intergroup contact in such situa-tions is essentially 'subsocial' in so far as the groups involved view each other as less than human in their intense struggle for re-sources (Frazier 1957:98). Previously unified societies may also, through colonial manipulation, be subject to severe organizational changes such as partition, aggravating intergroup violence (Fraser 1984). Whether traditional or contemporary in origin, colonialism may be viewed as the organized domination of one group by an-other in the context of migration based on vested economic mo-tives (Kinloch 1975:16).

The colonial model may be applied in a variety of ways: Carmichael and Hamilton (1967), for example, are well-known for their depiction of race relations in the United States as essentially 'colonial' in nature, with African Americans exploited as subjects requiring liberation from institutionalized racism. Blauner (1969) has also applied this concept to ghetto racial strife, underlining forced entry into the society, negative cultural consequences for minorities, institutionalized control, and racism as major factors behind black revolt. Groups subject to external colonialism may, in turn, colonize indigenous populations—the Indians in Mexico are a case in point, resulting in internal struggles for minority group independence (Casanova 1970). Colonial ghettos or enclaves may arise in rural settings as well, resulting in high levels of deprivation and dependence on external resources for subsistence (Dawkins & Kinloch 1975).

Different kinds of colonialism may also apply to the same minority: Moore (1970), for example, perceives Mexican Americans, depending on their region's particular history, as subject to 'classic,' 'conflict,' or 'economic' type of colonialism within the same society. In the first of these, the Mexicans of New Mexico represented an intact, indigenous elite which maintained its organizational resources. Those in Texas, however, were subject to the violence of revolutionary settlers, while migrant laborers in California experienced inconsistent immigration/deportation policies imposed by the state in response to changing economic conditions. Consequent political participation was highest in New Mexico and lowest in California, reflecting these differing internal colonial frontiers. The "celtic fringe" in Great Britain has also been conceptualized as a function of "internal colonialism," involving the superimposition of cultural differences on economic inequality, thereby reinforcing ongoing ethnic identities within the society as a whole (Hechter 1975). Colonialism may thus be either internal or external and affect the same minorities differently depending on particular contact situations. The consequences of this experience, however, are generally negative, resulting in highly competitive intergroup relations (van den Berghe 1974), characterized by dominant elites (Glick 1955), highly controlled multi-racial communities (Frazier 1957), and the use of negative stereotypes at all levels of society—individual, group, and institutional (Kinloch 1974). When minority group members are successful in rising to the middle class they tend to occupy "community service" positions predominantly (Hout 1986), while state organization at both local and national levels represents "local class structures," often revealing significant political differences by race (James 1988). As can be seen, the consequences of the colonial experience are generally negative, resulting in ongoing intergroup competition and conflict.

Finally, post-colonial situations are problematic also: emerging elites often consist of "metropolitan bourgeoisies" which reflect previous systems of domination and are largely unable to deal with the needs of the larger population they promised to serve. Consequently, former colonial elites continue to play significant

roles in this tense neo-colonial context (Mandazza 1986). Other analysts have also pointed to the "colonial heritage" as involving the
decline and failure of the central government in the wake of increasing decentralization and privatization of the society as a
whole. Again, such societies tend to be subject to the continuing
exploitation of (new) elites in a more fragmented and less organized societal environment (Rothchild & Chazon 1988). Post-independence situations may also reflect the increasing disillusion-
ment of the indigenous majority with their new governing elite's
lackluster ability to meet their rising political and economic expec-
tations (Kinloch 1997).

The above literature suggests a number of factors which may be
crucial to a comparative understanding of intergroup relations:
(1) societal conditions existing prior to intergroup contact (e.g., a
group's particular type or stage of European development), reflected in each population's desire to maintain its way of life (i.e.,
cultural continuity); (2) the types of elite involved, highlighting the
distinct difference between migrant and indigenous subordination
of minority populations; (3) elite types, in turn, tend to involve
varying contact situations, with migrant-indigenous experiences
proving significantly more negative and exploitive than indige-
nous-migrant situations; and (4) types of society and intergroup
relations vary accordingly, with migrant (often colonial)-ruled societies being significantly more discriminatory and conflict-ridden
than the (indigenous) non-colonial, with internal/external as well
as rural/urban colonialism, but varying by colonial origin. Such
"typical situations," however, are far from static. We turn to specify some factors making them dynamic over time.

Demographic Factors

Population characteristics have obvious relevance to intergroup
relations. Typically, colonial-type societies containing large, indigenous majorities are dominated by small, migrant elites (Lieberson 1961; Mason 1970; van den Berghe 1967), resulting in high
levels of violence and conflict (Spilerman 1970). Segregation, combined with institutionalized racism, tends to aggravate this situation and potential intergroup hostility (Kuper 1970; 1971; Spilerman 1970). Colonial elites tend to be highly insecure in such

situations and consequently conservative and rigid in their policies applied to subordinate minorities (Mason 1970). Racial disparities in educational, occupational, and economic achievement, furthermore, may vary over time but remain significant, nevertheless (Farley 1984). Ironically, significant improvement in such indices may also be associated with higher levels of protest and intergroup violence (Spilerman 1970). In any event, population characteristics and ratios are clearly related to intergroup definitions and relations.

Demographic dynamics, such as population growth, migration processes (including emigration and internal migration), and economic developments significantly modifying minority labor roles, may all affect such relations, increasing intergroup violence in some situations, as well as changing the views and reactions of both elites and subordinate minorities in others (Kinloch 1972; 1974). Demographic shifts, including population growth, economic differentiation, migration, and specialization, have also been linked to the emergence of highly complex types of minority group hierarchies involving racial, ethnic, economic, sexual, age-based, and behavioral inequality (Kinloch 1979:199). As populations change so do their needs and consequent social organization. As a result, intergroup relations are inevitably dynamic.

Other studies have highlighted the relevance of particular demographic factors to positive intergroup relations: democracies, for instance, tend to be culturally homogeneous and reflect high levels of industrialization and gross domestic product per capita (Lijphart 1984). Societies notable for their relative social harmony also tend to be relatively small, homogeneous, and hig' er in levels of economic development, education, and ecological density than more violent nations (Kinloch 1990). While it would be grossly naive to argue that economic development, aid, or modernization automatically produce more harmonious group relations, it is clear that high levels of material deprivation only aggravate a society's stratification situation, increasing potential intergroup hostility and violence among both elite and subordinate populations, whoever may be in power.

From the above discussion, it is clear that a society's population characteristics, combined with the types of economic and political organization within it, have a major impact on the its major types of intergroup relations. Furthermore, demographic, economic, and political change all work together as part of ongoing intergroup dynamics.

Ecological Factors

The ecological approach to intergroup relations focuses on the nature of initial and changing group *contact*. Of particular interest are the consequences of the kind of intergroup contact which initially takes place in a society's early formation based on interaction with outsiders. In the colonial situation, early interaction is often highly *negative*, as pointed out above, involving domination (Banton 1967), high levels of economic exploitation (Cox 1959), value differences (Schermerhorn 1964), significant levels of inequality and stratification (Bagley 1972; van den Berghe 1967), the creation of a variety of minorities (Mason 1970), and their subjection to segregation and exclusion by the colonial elite (Kinloch 1974). van den Berghe (1967) has also delineated a number of specific contacts which result in high levels of racism: military conquest, frontier expansion, and both voluntary and involuntary migration are typically involved (van den Berghe 1967:14). Others have highlighted the relevance of "European imperialism," "world capitalism," (Blue 1959), and those parts of the world subject to European dominance, external control, and the formation of multiracial communities (Frazier 1957).

Initial contacts on a worldwide level, however, vary from those promoting relative independence to others involving more direct colonial control and exploitation. These have been delineated as follows: (1) societies whose neutrality and/or independence have been guaranteed by larger and stronger nations; (2) countries ruled by monarchies who become constitutional monarchies, republics, democracies, or communist-ruled states (i.e., internal democratization); (3) nations formed primarily through external migration, particularly refugees who develop frontier and/or highly isolated societies (e.g., island plantations); (4) societies based largely on the manipulation of indigenous monarchies by outside elites who impose protectorate or colonial status on them through invasion and other forms of external control (i.e., forms of indirect colonialism); and (5) states formed through the direct colonial settlement and control of indigenous peoples by European elites (specifically, the French, British, Spanish, and Portuguese), including the imposed resolution of colonially-produced conflict through the partitioning process, effected largely by Great Britain (Kinloch 1993:178). Such a typology delineates a variety of contacts, ranging from those facilitating a society's relative independence, through the comparatively democratic, to those subject to indirect or direct colonial domination. The cumulative consequences of contact types are extremely powerful and relevant to ensuing intergroup relations within such *contexts*. These kinds of factors an also be used to appreciate the complexity of intra-societal relations. Migrant groups, for instance, may eventually establish and maintain themselves through future generations (Lieberson 1961:910). Contact situations, as in the United States, may proceed through a number of different stages with the same elite or minority variously occupying both migrant and indigenous positions, depending on the historical period involved. Consequently, contact situations may involve both negative and positive features, contingent on predominant circumstances.

Turning specifically to the United States, data continue to highlight the strong correlation between minority group status and socioeconomic achievement (Kinloch 1993:181): Asian Americans and whites are in the most advantaged position with respect to education, income, employment, and poverty with African Americans, Hispanics, Native Americans, Pacific Islanders, and Vietnamese Americans generally faring much worse in this regard. What do such statistics imply? Given the society was founded by a migrant, refugee elite, or exclusionary 'enlightenment' (Hartz 1964), this country represents a colonial-type situation, despite its overtly democratic nature. Accordingly, the society illustrates all the features of colonial contact: a migrant refugee elite, largely restricting democratic rights to whites, which subordinated the indigenous population, forcibly imported African Americans as slaves, appropriated parts of Mexico, and extended its empire to include other Pacific and Caribbean nations. Complicated by the voluntary/ refugee immigration of other ethnic and racial groups, American society consist of both indigenous and migrant types of intergroup contact, producing significant levels of conflict, discrimination, and inequality despite its high degree of general democracy. Conse-

quently, minorities with the least socioeconomic resources and subject to the most negative types of contact (Native Americans,
African Americans, many Hispanics, Pacific Islanders and Asian
refugees) reveal the highest levels of deprivation. However, groups
with greater educational and economic resources who enter the society under more voluntary and positive conditions (e.g., Chinese,
Japanese, Filipino, Asian Indian, Korean, and Cuban Americans)
fare significantly better, in some cases surpassing the white majority. In general, then, this society comprises both positive and negative intergroup contact situations with corollary types of intergroup
relations.

Contact situations or 'frontiers,' despite their stable and powerful consequences over time, are clearly dynamic rather than fixed
or static. In this regard, Park is well-known for his major contributions to social ecology, including his depiction of a race relations
cycle in which intergroup relations following initial domination inevitably consist of the dynamics of competition, conflict, and assimilation (Park 1950:104). These processes are implicit in the particular ecological situations or frontiers on which groups come
together, such as trading, plantation, political, urban, or tourist
(Lind 1969), making intergroup relations changing and dynamic.
This is reflected in fluctuating intergroup definitions, labels, and
political policies as a society's ecology changes with respect to its
economic, political, and consequent social ecology (Kinloch 1972).
In this manner, competition is viewed as endemic to any society, a
major force behind intergroup *dynamics.*

Competition and ensuing conflict may be viewed as major factors in all group processes. Realistic conflict theory specifies the
source of such conflict in the form of "incompatible group interests" based on the selfish goals of group members. This incompat-
ibility is viewed as the source of intergroup prejudice and hostility
and is reflected in Sumner's famous notion of ethnocentrism. Such
an approach may be applied to issues such as industrial unrest, international conflict, and school desegregation (Taylor & Moghaddam 1994).

Competition has also been applied to ethnicity in detail: increased rates of intergroup competition, produced by economic
change or policy developments such as desegregation, may reinforce ethnic boundaries and result in increased collective action

(Olzak 1992). This process also tends to be part of "ethnic adaptation" (Barth 1969), may be reflected in elite rivalry over state power (Brass 1985), and significantly strengthens group boundaries, as defined by rational choice theory (Banton 1983). In general, situations which become more apparently competitive inevitably reinforce group identity and boundaries as individuals members attempt to maximize their self-interest with respect to specific social policy issues such as housing and employment (Banton 1983). Ethnocentrism, prejudice, hostility, and conflict inevitably develop at the group level. As socioeconomic situations fluctuate, so will levels and types of intergroup conflict.

Using the ecological approach, then, societies may be compared, both internally and externally, with regard to their formative contact situations, changing frontiers over time, and manner in which intergroup competition affects group boundaries, collective action, and conflict. These factors are particularly relevant to understanding the (changing) contexts in which intergroup relations occur. We turn to specify the kinds of economic factors which influence these dynamics.

Economic Factors

Economic change may lead to a decline of traditional stratification systems (Shibutani & Kwan 1965), disturbing previous correlations between minority and economic status. As the relationship between caste and class is modified, "rank disequilibrium" or status inconsistency may emerge, producing heightened feelings of deprivation, social injustice, and intergroup hostility (Bagley 1970). Modernization may also reduce ethnic heterogeneity, resulting in increased ethnic mobilization, while increased labor market competition among ethnic groups may intensify "collective action" also (Olzak & Nagel 1986:17–46). Differing kinds of status disequilibrium may occur within the same social group, whether majority or minority, resulting in an assortment of potential reactions and social movements in any intergroup situation (Geschwender 1968; Spilerman 1970). High levels of status inconsistency and relative deprivation may also result eventually in a minority's rejection of a system of discrimination as totally illegitimate (Kinloch 1974:233–234; Taylor & Moghaddam 1994: chpt.7). Ethnic solidarity may also, under certain industrial circumstances, become the major basis for collective action, rather than other dimensions of minority group status, reflecting the manner in which modernization tends to highlight group cultural boundaries (Nielsen 1985). Market changes may reinforce group solidarity as well (Hechter 1987) while national growth may ironically result in particular resource scarcities, potentially increasing intergroup competition and violence (Choucri & North 1975). We have pointed out the manner in which democracies tend to possess high levels of industrialization, without assuming such a correlation is causal (Lijphart 1984). Runciman (1989), in a wide-ranging comparative analysis of nations as patterns of power, also focuses on underlying economic factors, particularly industrialization, in his delineation of industrial nation-states as liberal-democratic, authoritarian, state socialist and apartheid-type societies.

Colonial economies tend to be particularly discriminatory, given their elite exploitation of minorities as labor resources. Major features such as dual labor markets (Bonacich 1976), middleman minorities (Bonacich & Modell 1980), as well as low social mobility, lack of educational and economic opportunities, and low political participation (Francis 1976) all tend to increase ethnic prominence and rebellion against these forms of institutionalized domination.

In general, then, financial dynamics may modify minority economic status, increase intergroup competition, reduce ethnic heterogeneity, underlie particular types of state power, and provoke factions to mobilize to protect their interests and oppose elite domination. These processes are vital to changing contact situations and consequent intergroup dynamics. Bringing together a society's major population characteristics, formative contact situations, changing frontiers, and economic dynamics offers the researcher important comparative insight into varying types of intergroup relations. Before applying these factors to our analysis, however, we need to specify some additional and important elements.

Sociocultural Factors

Significant sociocultural variables include the following: elite values, motives, and origins; value differences and consequent conflict with subordinate minorities; processes involved in cultural contacts among groups; and the culture of conflict or relative harmony. The values of migrant elite tend to be highly ethnocentric and exploitive, often WASP (White, Anglo-Saxon Protestant) and exclusive (Kinloch 1974; Noel 1968), highly expansionistic (Kennedy 1971), and expressed in power relationships with all minorities in the society (Bonilla 1968). Non-Wasp cultures are also highly domineering but tend to be more accepting of subordinate and often indigenous minorities (Degler 1971). Within societies, elite priorities produce a prestige hierarchy of groups ranked by their degree of similarity to those values (Kinloch 1974). Sociocultural phenomena, accordingly, represent a very powerful part of any country's social organization.

We have also emphasized an elite's historical origins in the case of 'fragment' societies, highlighting the particular stage of European history from which they "broke off:" feudal, liberal, and radical (Hartz 1964). These views are also driven by a conservative desire to maintain their 'origins' in a foreign environment. Accordingly, a migrant elite's particular *motives* reflect their particular origins and have a major impact on the type of society they form on colonial arrival, with powerful historical continuity from that point on. In general, their aims are exploitive in such situations, rationalized by the particular sub-cultural values they bring with them. The indigenous populations they conquer and the groups they import, forcibly or otherwise, are defined in the context of these mores applied in an ethnocentric manner.

Migrant/indigenous values also differ significantly in the colonial context, with the former typically representing western, industrial, materialistic, individualistic orientations in contrast to the generally opposite concerns of indigenous cultures. This value conflict and its "cumulative directionality" (Schermerhorn 1964) play a major role in the colonial situation, particularly in subsequent power relations, legitimacy beliefs, and types of intergroup relations. Accordingly, intergroup conflict, while involving significant power differentials, fundamentally represents the clash of cultures in particular situations.

Taking this approach, intergroup settings involve *culture contacts* and associated processes such as ethnocentric prejudice and stereotyping, cultural assimilation as defined by social ecologists such as

Park (1950), and the ever-present potential for ethnic mobilization in threatening and competitive situations (Barth 1969). Since all groups are "culture bearing" (Barth 1969), representing their particular environmental adaptation, changing resource situations and arrangements make the possibility of group dynamics becoming ethnic dynamics constant in any society. Accordingly, group boundaries may be reinforced by ethnic mobilization at any time.

The manner in which a society deals with conflict is also very relevant to the kinds of intergroup relations which occur within it. Some cultures, for example, are clearly more organized to deal with conflict in a relatively peaceful manner than others (Ross 1993). In this regard, colonial societies tend to be founded on violence and perpetuate such a tradition in their reaction to conflict, rebellion, or hostility. The United States, with its frontier tradition, for instance, reveals a "culture of violence" in its colonial foundation, westward expansion, slavery tradition, and destructive reaction to conflict within it. Other colonial societies, particularly those in South and Central America, reveal similarly negative environments, resulting in massacres, often on a large scale, when minorities rebel. Accordingly, the manner in which elite values may become institutionalized in a destructive way often plays a significant role in the manner intergroup conflict is 'resolved.' The need to explore and organize more peaceful and harmonious modes of conflict resolution becomes urgent in such settings. Often positive role models in this regard are lacking or largely absent in these situations. The establishment of constructive traditions becomes an urgent necessity to avoid destructive consequences.

Major sociocultural factors involved in intergroup relations, then, include elite values, motives, and origins, the kinds of value conflicts which often occur in intergroup contact, the dynamics of inter-cultural processes, and the culture of violence typical of colonial situations. We turn next to the political contexts in which they operate.

Political Factors

Relevant political factors include elite orientations, the formation and use of state power, dynamics of ethnic mobilization, globalization of politics, as well as the importance of self-determination and constructive conflict-resolution. We have already pointed to the exploitive, conservative motives of migrant elites. These are often translated politically into defensive, 'siege'-like cultures when responding to perceived insecurity or attack (Baker 1974, 1975). In these kinds of situations, protection of elite interests at all costs becomes paramount, potentially resulting in disastrous levels of violence and "battles to the end." Colonial politics become desperate attempts by elites to protect their interests, including adapting to changing economic and political environments in ways designed to maintain their control of the society (Kinloch 1987). While arguments and policies may vary over time, these racial or ethnic politics tend to reflect these conservative dynamics.

The kinds of states which have emerged out of the decline of empires have also been highly problematic, often involving the external manipulation and consolidation of a variety of minorities for political purposes. Frequently, they have resulted in high levels of ethnic conflict (Bell & Freeman 1974; Brass, 1985; Rabie 1994; Ryan 1990), low levels of self-determination (Klein & Reban 1981), and rising levels of state power (Meyer & Hannan 1979). We have also commented on the continuing kinds of intergroup problems evident in post-colonial situations, in which neo-colonial elites further their own interests often to the detriment of the larger society (Kinloch 1997; Mandazza 1986). Thus, post-independence constitutions and actual power arrangements tend to reflect their historical antecedents.

In these kinds of political settings, many political dynamics represent ethnic responses to various kinds of deprivation, often economic (Pinard 1971). Gurr and Harff (1994) have, perhaps, developed one of the most comprehensive explanations of ethnic mobilization as representing a complex of factors: ethnic group discrimination; group identity; ethnic group cohesion; political environment; government violence; external support; and a regime's international status are together behind levels of "ethnopolitical violence" (1994:77–114). Central to their approach are the two factors of discrimination and ethnic identity, viewing ethnic responses to discrimination in particular contexts as vital to the understanding of consequent conflict. Some societal situations, internally and externally, are more conflict-prone than others. Others have also attempted to account for "collective action" as responses to discriminatory stratification, changing mobility, and consequent "consciousness raising" (Taylor & McKirnan 1984). Again, political activities represent group responses to discrimination and inequality in the larger society. Since many societies contain significant levels of such deprivation, the potential for ethnic politics is ever-present.

The context in which ethnic strife occurs has also become increasingly *global,* resulting in the emergence of multi-national movements and increasing relevance of international rather than national politics (Luard 1990). Organizations such as the United Nations, furthermore, have become increasingly involved directly in peace-keeping operations and the resolution of potentially violent situations, shifting from a relatively passive to more reactive role in the world arena. Recent examples include situations in Haiti, Somalia, Bosnia, and Iraq. Dynamic coalitions on the world stage have become a dominant feature of attempts to deal with intergroup violence, occasionally in genocidal proportions, in this increasingly international setting. Crucial within this is the need to adequately understand and facilitate conflict-resolution on a long-term basis (Burton 1990; Ryan 1990). This includes the peace-making, building, and keeping activities of third parties (Ryan 1990), a fuller understanding of the political relationships behind such conflict, crucial distinction between conflict settlement and resolution, and need to institutionalize such solutions (Burton 1990). Particularly crucial in all of this is dealing effectively with any group's claims to 'self-determination' or independence—essentially the *opposite* of the colonial situation (Bell & Freeman 1974; Halperin, Scheffer & Small 1992). Since lack of such freedom is a major factor behind intergroup violence, facilitating group independence represents a major part of effective conflict-resolution.

Relevant political factors, then, include elite motives and orientations, the formation and use of state power, ethnic mobilization as a response to discrimination, increasing globalization of politics generally, and crucial importance of facilitating self-determination as a prime method of conflict-resolution. We turn finally to more individual or psychological factors affecting intergroup relations.

Psychological Factors

Our discussion has largely focused on factors operating on the societal and group level: historical, demographic, ecological, economic, sociocultural, and political variables are not particularly individualistic. However, this is *not* to suggest that intergroup relations ignore a person's relatively unique traits. We are all socialized and interact in particular social environments, reacting to them in our own ways. Highly discriminatory and/or violent settings have powerful effects on individuals. Feelings of victimization and the need to defend one's sense of self may be an important part of violence at the group level (Montville 1990). Some situations may be particularly 'emotion-laden,' resulting in a need for "emotional cleansing." (Taylor & Moghaddam 1994:202–203).

Social identity theory also highlights the manner in which as individuals we have strong social identities, causing us to value and protect our in-groups in opposition to out-groups (Taylor & Moghaddam 1994:61–94). We also "strive for justice" or 'equity' in our relationships with others and are upset by perceived injustice (Taylor & Moghaddam 1994: 97). Thirdly, we evaluate our "relative status" in life in reference to our feelings of satisfaction or dissatisfaction, rather than feeling automatically deprived by our general status in society (Taylor & Moghaddam 1994:119). As individuals, then, we have strong *group identities* which we strive to protect, make equitable, and evaluate relative to other social units in the larger society. Such bonds may be important elements in our changing levels of intergroup hostility, ethnocentrism, and potential conflict, particularly in highly discriminatory and changing situations.

High levels of prejudice and aggressive behavior have also been related to psychological phenomena. The Freudian tradition, for example, is reflected in approaches focusing on the dynamics of frustration and aggression as well as particular personality types, including the 'authoritarian' and 'prejudiced' (Taylor & Moghaddam 1994: 17–33; Kinloch 1974:58–70). While these approaches tend to underestimate the relevance of the social context to interpersonal attitudes and behavior, they are useful in linking the individual's emotional dependence on prejudice to highly discriminatory forms of behavior under conditions of overt intergroup competition and social change. Perceived external hierarchies and their assumed legitimacy may be very important to an individual's sense of self in highly stratified and changing societies. While personality factors may not figure greatly in highly racist societies with very prejudiced norms (Pettigrew 1958; Kinloch 1974), they may become salient in any situation containing increased levels of competition and changing social policies such as desegregation. In general, then, individual emotions, personality factors and social identities are important elements in intergroup relations also.

We turn finally to relate the above factors to different types of intergroup relations.

Comparative Intergroup Relations

This analysis has highlighted a number of factors behind varying types of intergroup relations: (1) group *motives* prior to contact; (2) each group's *desire* for socioeconomic and cultural *continuity* reflected in the kinds of social organization set up after intergroup contact; and (3) the major distinction between *two types of contact situations* (migrant/indigenous and indigenous/migrant), highlighting two types of elite—migrant (i.e., refugee, indirect, and direct colonial elites) and indigenous elites (societies whose independence is guaranteed by outsiders or have experienced the internal democratization of traditional monarchies).[2]

The major historical, ecological, economic, sociocultural, political, psychological, and consequent intergroup relations differences between these two types of contact situation are outlined in Table 4.1. Here the comparative differences between these two general types of intergroup relations are clear: *indigenous rulers* tend to be *large, less competitive and manipulative, creating more harmonious societal settings and social relations. Migrant elites,* on the other hand, are *smaller, more exploitive, ethnocentric, manipulative, and discriminatory, resulting in very negative intergroup situations and dynamics.* While applicable to societies as a whole, such an approach may also be applied to the varying kinds of *contact situations* within the same nation, reflecting regional and varying historical situations within it.

This typology also suggests a more general model of intergroup relations: these *dynamics* involve a society's internal levels of conflict, group formation, types of power, and ongoing demographic characteristics. They are also produced and influenced by a complex of factors: the particular *historical circumstances* in which groups come into contact with each other (i.e., types of elite/subor-

Table 4.1 Types of Societal Elites and Intergroup Relations

Factors	Indigenous Elites	Migrant Elites
Historical	larger elites	small elites
	more unified societies	fragment societies
	less conservative elites	conservative elites
	lower elite ethnocentrism	high elite ethnocentrism
	lower elite exploitation	high elite exploitation
	more positive intergroup contact	negative intergroup contact
	lower levels of competition	high levels of competition
	lower group diversity	high group diversity
Demographic	lower segregation and discrimination	high segregation and discrimination
	less complex minority hierarchy	increasingly complex minority hierarchy
Ecological	more positive intergroup contact	negative intergroup contact
	higher minority independence	low minority independence
	competition generally does not result in collective action	competition results in collective action
Economic	more unified labor markets	segmented labor markets
	generally absent	middleman minorities
	high G.N.P.	low G.N.P.
Sociocultural	more positive elite values/motives	negative elite values/motives
	lower intergroup value conflict	high intergroup value conflict
	lower intergroup cultural conflict	high intergroup cultural conflict
Political	more majority politics	elite politics
	non-siege elite mentalities	elite siege mentalities
	generally absent	elite state manipulation
	generally absent	ethnic response to deprivation
	more democratic	low democracy
Psychological	generally absent	minority feelings of victimization/need for emotional cleansing
	lower minority group identites	high minority group identities
	lower frustration-aggression	high frustration-aggression
	less prejudiced personalities	highly prejudiced personalities

(continues)

Table 4.1   *(continued)*

Factors	Indigenous Elites	Migrant Elites
Intergroup relations	lower levels of intergroup conflict	high levels of intergroup conflict
	indigenous social arrangements	imposed social arrangements
	lower minority unity and conflict	high minority unity and conflict
	lower elite domination of society	high elite domination of society
	low internal colonialism	high internal colonialism
	not applicable	negative post-colonial consequences
	high levels of indigenous groups	decline of indigenous groups
	higher minority economic assimilation	low minority economic assimilation
	controlled immigration	high levels of immigration

dinate situations); their *demographic* characteristics (e.g., group size, minorities created, structural arrangements regarding segregation and discrimination); *ecological* contexts (types of contact, competition, conflict, accommodation, etc.); *economic* dynamics (e.g., types of labor markets, minority economic/labor roles, types of economic development); *sociocultural* features (particularly elite values and cultural interaction with minorities); *political* features (elite power arrangements, reactions, and minority responses); and related *psychological* characteristics (particularly the emotional reactions of majority and minority group members). According to this approach, intergroup relations reflect the kinds of social interaction which occur within these particular settings, their interrelationship, and continuing dynamics, i.e., they take place in particular combinations of specific *contexts* (historical, demographic, ecological, economic, sociocultural, political, and psychological) and result in distinctive types of interaction (i.e., levels and types of conflict and/or discrimination). More generally, *particular kinds of historical contact situations* involve *varying types of elites, treatment of minorities, economic arrangements, political mentalities, individual emotions, and consequent types of intergroup relations,* i.e., contact situations are crucial for their *historical continuity* as societal contexts in which particular kinds of social relations are likely to occur. Furthermore, societies founded and dominated by migrant elites tend to be much more problematic than those ruled by indigenous groups: the former often involve small, conservative, ethnocentric elites who experience negative contact with other groups, segregating and exploiting them economically. Minorities, in turn, experience high levels of frustration and feelings of victimization. Consequently, intergroup relations tend to be highly conflict-ridden and problematic on a long-term basis. Countries ruled by indigenous majorities, on the other hand, tend to be more positive regarding elite and minority attitudes and characteristics. Intergroup relations are generally more harmonious as a result. While the typology delineated above is regarded as neither exclusive nor exhaustive, it should prove useful as an analytical starting-point in analyzing the kinds of factors relevant to intergroup relations on a number of levels and situations. The remainder of this monograph involves applying this model to intergroup dynamics within the United States specifically and the rest of the world at large to gain detailed insight into how they operate.

Notes

1. Parts of this chapter are based on the author's paper, "The Comparative Analysis of Intergroup Relations: An Exploration," published in the *International Journal of Contemporary Sociology* 30, 1993:173–184. I am very grateful to the *Journal's* editor for permission to use it in this manner.

2. cf. Lieberson (1961).

PART TWO

Intergroup Relations Within the United States

5

Intergroup Relations Within the United States: Introduction

The United States is often thought of as a liberal democracy, an open society or meritocracy, in which an individual is free to pursue his or her dream unfettered by artificial barriers or types of discrimination. As the "land of opportunity," this society is viewed positively as one of the world's greatest industrial democracies. The reality, of course, is rather different: while limited minority progress has been made during recent decades, the continuing impact of race, ethnicity, gender, class and other dimensions of inequality is clearly evident in differential poverty and incarceration levels. Enduring signs of stereotyping and prejudice are also visible in the form of hate crimes, militia behavior, and everyday expressions of bigotry, highlighting the persistent operation of minority group stratification in this country.

Why is this so? Contrary to the cultural myth of American democracy, this society is clearly *colonial* in nature (i.e., settled by an external, migrant elite), particularly when viewed in relation to its historical foundation, cultural values, and demographic/economic development. This section of our analysis examines these factors in the U.S. case, delineates their impact on intergroup relations within the society, and compares varying colonial contexts on the state level, illustrating a *colonial continuum* based on varying kinds of historical group contact.

America's Colonial Context

As is well-known, North America was once the home of hundreds of Indian tribes with varying languages, cultures, and political systems. While some have become extinct, their total numbers continue to increase significantly, despite the harsh treatment they have experienced in this society (Nagel 1996). Their broad cultural variety has ensured their lack of political unity; nevertheless, they have all been subject to similarly negative and destructive treatment by the invading colonists.

As emphasized, the major features of American society are significantly *colonial:* founded by a *migrant,* minority elite of white Protestants, the indigenous Indian population was *subordinated,* segregated into reservations subject to ongoing control and manipulation, and, in some cases, experienced attempted extermination. The WASP elite also *appropriated* much of their land and even tried to exploit the resources assigned to them. Requiring labor to exploit their economic interests, the colonial elite proceeded to *import* other minorities, either forcibly or on a somewhat voluntary basis, subjecting them to continuing *prejudice* and *discrimination.* From this it is clear that the American case reflects all the major elements of the colonial process: migration, subordination, exploitation, importation, and discrimination (Kinloch 1974).

A major factor in this situation are the values of the colonial elite, conceptualized in the form of the *Protestant Ethic.* So-called 'mainstream' American values consist largely of an emphasis on puritanism, moralism, individualism, materialism, and the moral significance of hard work. These orientations are narrow, exclusive, and highly intolerant, reflecting significant levels of ethnocentrism—a major factor behind prejudice and discrimination generally. Minorities viewed as culturally similar to the WASP elite are subject to less prejudice than those defined as very different and therefore inferior. Furthermore, the narrowness and exclusive nature of these values reinforces the elite's resistant and conservative reaction to social change, defining such events as threatening to their interests and consequently those of the society as a whole. Responses to attempted power modifications in intergroup relations tend to be resistant or generally negative. Given the religious or puritan context in which these values were historically founded, their inherent ethnocentrism is rationalized in powerful religious terms, typified historically in the notion of "manifest destiny"— the presumption of divinely ordained conquest and superiority over subordinated minorities. Consequently, colonial dominance is defined as divinely inspired and rationalized accordingly. While these supporting arguments have become secularized in the form of maintaining the "American way of life," they remain highly exclusive in effect, reinforcing the colonial elite's presumption of superiority and 'right' to dominance. Establishment reactions to minority demands for equality range from harsh denial to mild accommodation, depending on how secure the former feel their interests are at the time. Furthermore, while some groups may be viewed as more 'acceptable' than others in cultural terms, they remain outside ingroup boundaries to a large extent, permitting the colonial elite to conserve its power and privileged position.

The structure of inequality based on such attitudes was clearly designed to favor the colonial elite, discriminating against others in a number of political, economic, and social ways. Indigenous groups have largely been excluded from the larger society while others, depending on their cultural features and resources, have been assigned limited positions or roles in the stratification hierarchy according to their historical circumstances, differentiated particularly according to whether they are 'colonized' or 'immigrant' minorities (McLemore & Romo 1998). The former tend to have fared worse than the latter, depending on the situations under which they entered the U.S. Groups who enter the society under more positive conditions, possess educational, occupational, and economic resources, and are physically and culturally similar to the white elite tend to fare much better than those who immigrate under more negative circumstances (Kinloch 1974). Consequently, in such a context, *institutionalized inequality* represents the context in which intergroup relations occur in the society, reflecting elite interests and attitudes.

Implicit within this colonial situation are a complex of largely *negative* contact situations or *historical frontiers*. Beginning with the destructive colonial frontier, eventually involving intergroup conflict, violence, and dominance, subsequent settings have included plantation situations, internal and external war experiences, periods of economic change and stress, and decades during which major political developments have taken place, both within and outside the society. Significant in all of this is the largely competitive and negative character of these types of intergroup situations. While this does not imply that positive developments were completely absent, it underlines the largely conflict-prone nature of colonial intergroup relations.

Finally, implicit in these frontiers is their *historical continuity:* Native Americans remain largely segregated in their reservations, others continue to live in urban ghettos, many recall their negative historical treatment, while a number of minorities continue to occupy negative occupational and economic positions in the society generally. Throughout all of this, the colonial elite maintains its position of political and economic dominance, demanding that minorities conform totally to its way of life or remain largely excluded. The 1990's are based on an economic rather than social mentality, reflecting a return to earlier levels of individualism, competition, prejudice, and reversal of policies designed to significantly reduce discrimination (i.e., affirmative action). Everyday expressions of racial intolerance and bigotry are clearly more evident also in frequent and violent "hate crimes" directed against particular groups such as gays and racial minorities.

The above discussion has highlighted a number of features typical of the *colonial situation:* the dynamics of migration, subordination, and importation, narrow and exclusive Protestant Ethic elite values, institutionalized inequality designed to serve elite interests, negative historical frontiers within which intergroup relations have occurred, and the historical continuity of competitive, negative intergroup contact. What are the consequences of these features for intergroup relations generally? We turn to this topic next in our discussion.

Colonial Intergroup Relations

How do the colonial features of American society define intergroup relations within it? They clearly occur within a well-defined *structure* founded on race, elaborated by ethnicity and class, further subdivided by gender, age, and deviance (Kinloch 1979). Such dimensions reflect the society's historical foundation, colonial culture, migration patterns, and economic development over time. Race operates with respect to the white-non-white axis, within which ethnic differences have emerged primarily out of voluntary migration into the society. Race also reflects class-based stratification reflecting particular historical and economic situations, particularly minority labor roles. In turn, race, ethnicity, and class all tend to be sub-differentiated by gender, age-based, and behaviorally-defined inequalities. Such a hierarchy also tends to be highly *integrated*, with race, ethnicity, and class defining the operation of discrimination at lower levels, e.g., they *mediate* the influence of gender, age, and behavior-based types of inequality (Kinloch 1979).

Within this hierarchy, an individual's *personal status* is defined by his or her majority-minority membership configuration. The higher a person is on each dimension (i.e., the closer they are to being white, WASP, upper-class, male, non-deviant adults) the more status and power they generally possess. Since this hierarchy is highly integrated, individual profile memberships tend to be cumulative, with higher order statuses potentially overriding the disadvantages associated with minority group status lower in the structure. Conversely, lower level group memberships tend to aggravate the kinds of disadvantages associated with them. Each type of status, furthermore, may involve a number of levels and types of inequality within it. Varying status combinations are also behind both implicit and explicit intergroup competition depending on particular social situations. Also, these status elements define intergroup relations at all levels of society, particularly in the case of majority-minority interaction.

Particular *societal needs* also operate within this hierarchy from the top down. Thus, the economic significance of race (exploitive labor roles), ethnicity (specialized labor roles also), and class (labor and consumption functions) tend to define the psychological or emotional significance of gender and age (the ego-needs of males and adults in relation to females, children, and the aged) and normative or moralistic definition of behavioral minorities as 'deviant' and therefore inferior. In this manner, all of society's major needs or functions are served within its hierarchy of inequality in a manner which clearly favors the power majority or elite (Kinloch 1979).

These exploitive functions require elaborate and powerful *legitimation*, accomplished primarily through *religion* and *science*. The former is particularly implicit within the Protestant Ethic with its presumption of exclusive elite moralistic superiority, civilization, righteousness, and elect membership, reflected in views of all minorities as inferior, less developed, un-American, weak, stupid, irrational, and immoral in some fashion. Science has often been used to highlight assumed intergroup *differences* and therefore presumed *inferiorities* on occasion, particularly when situations are viewed as problematic in *some* fashion. Depicting a minority's presumed physical, cultural, intellectual, emotional, and behavioral deficiencies as biologically or genetically-fixed and/or ordained by God represents an extremely powerful and deterministic form of intergroup stereotyping and prejudice. Since this society places such a high emphasis on both institutions, the enduring, pervasive nature of bigotry within it is hardly surprising.

This hierarchy is far from static: *dynamic processes* such as internal and external migration, economic development and change, urbanization, and ecological dynamics all modify intergroup boundaries and interrelations. New minorities may form, others may decline, while both majorities and minorities change in their reactions to each other over time. Subordinate groups demand greater equality and rights under some circumstances while elite reaction may range from the more liberal and accommodationist to the more reactionary, depending on perceived economic, political, and social circumstances. In this society, race, ethnic, class, and gender relations have been particularly dynamic in this fashion. However, the above hierarchy remains largely *stable* and in place, despite such variations, reflecting the elite's generally *conservative* response to attacks on its vested interests. Inequality remains institutionalized in a manner which protects majority economic, political, and moral resources.

In general, American intergroup relations occur within an integrated hierarchy, within which individual social status is defined by majority-minority group membership in a cumulative fashion. This structure serves a broad range of majority or elite functions, rationalized in religious and scientific terms. Intergroup boundaries and relations within it vary over time as the society experiences demographic, economic, and ecological change; nevertheless, the hierarchy remains large stable over time, tied to the elite's protection of its interests and conservative response to significant social change. Bringing these features together, it appears reasonable to depict colonial intergroup relations generally as defined by an integrated, cumulative hierarchy, subject to religious and scientific rationalization, and influenced by social change but in a manner which preserves its general form and elite dominance over time. Individual and group interaction, while involving psychological and attitudinal elements, should nevertheless be understood within this *structural context* and its associated levels and types of power. Finally, this hierarchy has been produced by the *colonial process*, particularly the kinds of historical and continuing *intergroup contacts* within it.

It would be a mistake to assume, however, that American intergroup relations are homogeneous throughout the society; rather, each state involves particular types of group contact along a *colonial continuum*. The United States consists of a variety of intergroup contact situations: (1) isolated and less colonial areas, i.e., those less accessible to colonial dominance and exploitation; (2) states initially controlled by adjacent powers, particularly Mexico; (3) those dominated by invading white majorities; and, (4) the most colonial, involving slavery and high levels of consequent racial conflict. We shall examine these in the chapters to follow.

Conclusions

The United States clearly represents a *colonial context* in which the indigenous population was subordinated, stripped of most of its resources and power, and relegated to largely excluded regions of the country. Other minorities were imported for labor to exploit the land so acquired, some forcibly, others on a more 'voluntary' basis, but all have been subject to stereotyping and discrimination. In this context, the largely W.A.S.P. elite, driven by narrow, intolerant Protestant ethic-type values, have set up a society designed to serve their own interests largely, reflecting the above history of negative frontiers, resulting in the formation of a clearly defined majority/minority group hierarchy, and serving a range of economic, psychological, and normative functions, rationalized by science and religion. While inherently dynamic, such an environment is subject to the elite's resistance to any kind of social change perceived as potentially threatening its privileged position.

Such a context, while generally homogeneous with regard to its power hierarchy, varies in the levels and kinds of *colonial contacts* within it by state and region: some, given their relative isolation, have experienced more moderate kinds of colonial contact; others have been subject to the formative influences of neighboring powers; a significant number have been invaded and controlled by relatively homogeneous white majorities; while the remainder have encountered all the major elements of colonialism in their contemporary formation, including forcible importation of minorities with extremely destructive consequences. Consequently, intergroup relations within this colonial society vary in accordance with their formative colonial experiences: the *more features of the colonial process they have been subject to, the more conflict-ridden such relations tend to be.* We turn to examine these varying contexts in the chapters to follow.

6

Intergroup Relations Within the United States: The Less Colonial

We begin our analysis with an examination of less colonial areas within the country: the more isolated and less accessible to colonial exploitation; and states initially controlled by neighboring powers such as Spain or Mexico. These tend to involve situations in which fewer features of the colonial process have come into play.

Isolated and Less Colonial Situations

Alaska, Hawaii, and Puerto Rico represent highly isolated or island settings in which intergroup conflict has been relatively low since colonial domination was established. In essence, they involve external territories subject to relatively low levels of colonialism. Given their location, outside domination took place gradually over time, their populations were often ethnically diverse, intergroup relations have been fairly peaceful, their economies tended to involve mining, agriculture, and increasingly tourism, their cultures were pluralistic, politically they evolved through territory to statehood status (except in the case of Puerto Rico), and they have experienced relatively low levels of intergroup conflict and psychological 'need' for violence. In general, they were founded on comparatively limited types of external migration, control, and domination.

Alaska was settled by a Russian trading company in the eighteenth century and was purchased by the United States the following century. Its history was relatively unique in a number of respects: early establishment of civil authority, self-rule, female suffrage, outlawing of racial discrimination in accommodation, and significant indigenous land settlements (Antonson & Hanable 1984). The state also experienced significant economic development in the form of an early gold rush, later oil production, and more recently, a tourist boom. Its population is also ethnically diverse, highlighting a variety of indigenous and immigrant groups. While whites may be in the majority, the state is both racially and ethnically pluralistic. Finally, the state has experienced relatively low levels of intergroup conflict. Clearly, this region is one of the more unique in the country. The state is distinctive for its early self-rule, establishment of civil rights, economic success, and relative social harmony in the context of diversity. As a frontier region in a relatively isolated, inaccessible part of the country, the state has developed in its own, relatively unique fashion.

Hawaii represents another unusual isolated case: the Islands were ruled by an indigenous monarch during much of early contact with outsiders, eventually overthrown in a peaceful coup (Lind 1969). Much of early intergroup contact was peaceful and somewhat equalitarian, with colonial takeover relentless but a gradual and bloodless process. Plantations were eventually established and largely worked by outside immigrant contract labor. The area eventually became a U.S. territory and state, during which World War II hastened the assimilation of many groups, particularly the Japanese, into the larger culture. Known for its official norm of nonracism and high levels of racial intermarriage among a broad diversity of racial groups, Hawaii represents one of the most relatively unique patterns of race relations (Kinloch 1974). Its economy is diverse and strong, particularly with respect to tourism, while its ethnic diversity remains one of the highest worldwide. This is *not* to suggest intergroup conflict has never occurred: strike-related riots and racial tension, particularly after Pearl Harbor, clearly occurred. Racial attitudes also reveal a hierarchy based on group socioeconomic hierarchy (Kinloch 1973). However, the state's intergroup relations remain largely harmonious and this society is relatively unique in a number of respects: its history of fairly peaceful intergroup contact, gradual external domination, significant economic development, emphasis on attitudinal tolerance, and high levels of interracial mixture. While limited in other respects, this state remains one of the most unusual in the United States, if not the world. Clearly subject to economic and demographic pressures, these islands are still one of the most unique areas of the society and will remain so.

Puerto Rico, an island commonwealth and not a state, is significant for its predominant Hispanic population, history of external rather than internal conflict (many other colonial nations attacked the area, Spain, France, Great Britain, and the Netherlands included), eventual cession to the United States, early abolition of slavery (particularly in the case of Catholics), and a highly developed plantation and recent tourist economy (Golding 1973). Its population remains largely Hispanic, African, Indian and Roman Catholic. While there have been significant outbreaks of anti-U.S. protests and violence, intergroup relations in this situation have not been highly destructive generally-speaking. Again, this society stands out in a number of ways: most of its conflict has been externally-generated, slavery was abolished early in its history, its take-over was relatively gradual, and its population, in contrast to Alaska and Hawaii, is very homogeneous. While the debate concerning statehood continues, the state remains an important part of the U.S. culturally and economically.

The comparative typology developed in chapter 4 delineated a number of dimensions related to intergroup dynamics: historical, demographic, ecological, economic, sociocultural, political, and psychological. Applying these to Alaska, Hawaii, and Puerto Rico, these cases appear generally to involve peaceful, gradual patterns of domination, high levels of (non-white) diversity, relatively positive contact frontiers over time, significant levels of economic development and change, often based on non-indigenous labor, sociocultural pluralism, and limited (often sporadic and/or external) types and levels of intergroup conflict. These *isolated* situations reflect relatively *low levels of colonialism*, consequently producing limited degrees and types of conflict. These contexts clearly represent particular types of external migration, exploitation, and migration, somewhat more typical of indigenous/migrant rather than migrant/indigenous based societies. They tend to illustrate that situations founded on gradual, relatively peaceful domination in pluralistic contexts, reinforced by positive continuing contact frontiers, result in more harmonious types of intergroup relations for the most part. This is *not* to argue that conflict is absent, nor that they are free of significant levels of inequality and other social problems; rather, as particular types of social contexts, they appear to have more positive intergroup consequences. In these cases, relatively *low levels of colonialism* tend to result in *more positive intergroup relations* generally. These cases are summarized in Table 6.1, highlighting these features: taken as a whole, they tend to reflect progressive rather than sudden colonial dominance, demographic heterogeneity, fairly positive historical frontiers, strong economies, and relatively low levels of intergroup conflict.

States Initially Controlled by Adjacent Powers

Arizona, California, Colorado, New Mexico, Nevada, and Texas represent states originally part of and/or subject to the control of external powers such as Spain or Mexico. Many of them were once part of the latter, eventually ceded to the United States. Obviously, they continue to involve high rates of ethnic and religious diversity, particularly Catholic Hispanics. Such initial, adjacent external control and pluralism has mediated the process of American colonialism in these cases, limiting the process largely to external migration, restricted subordination of indigenous groups, and largely voluntary immigration. While some of these contexts contain a variety of other minorities, intergroup conflict has largely involved historical violence against Native Americans, the creation of reservations for them, and the immigration of African Americans in *some* cases, particularly Colorado (where the KKK was active) and California (which has experienced race riots, significant white violence, and the recent reversal of affirmative action policies.

Arizona was subject to both Spanish and Mexican rule, and eventually ceded to the United States during the nineteenth century. Significant levels of white-Native American violence occurred, with massacres on both sides. A large number of Indian reservations were established with later attempts to provide educational facilities (Faulk 1970). Japanese American internment occurred during 1942, with Native Americans granted the franchise later that decade. The state also contains a fairly large Hispanic population, many of Mexican origin. While significant levels of

Table 6.1 Isolated and Less Colonial Situations

Cases	Historical	Demographic	Ecological	Economic	Sociocultural	Political	Psychological
Alaska	Early self-rule, decline of discrimination	High indigenous populations	Limited intergroup conflict	High economic development	High diversity	Self-rule, territory, state	Relatively low intergroup conflict
Hawaii	Monarchy, treaty, monarchy overthrow	High racial, ethnic diversity	Relatively peaceful	High economic development	High diversity	Territory, state	Relatively low intergroup conflict
Puerto Rico	Spanish control, external attacks, cession to USA, territory	Relatively homogenous	External conflict	High economic development	Low diversity	Territory, commonwealth	Relatively low intergroup conflict

colonial-indigenous violence occurred in its early history, civil rights and relative intergroup harmony were more frequent in later periods. Consequently, this state exemplifies medium levels of colonialism illustrated in external migration, indigenous subordination and resource expropriation, later immigration, and limited levels of intergroup conflict. Early contact violence, later civil rights, and limited levels of intergroup conflict typify its general historical development.

New Mexico was also subject to Spanish and Mexican rule, ceded to the United States in 1848. White conflict with both Native Americans and Mexicans took place over the decades, with the former obtaining the vote in 1948 and significant land grants later in the century. Hispanics represent a significant proportion of the state's population, many descended from early Spanish settlers (Larson 1968). According to Moore (1970), they have been subject to 'classic' colonialism, maintaining their indigenous elite largely intact, resulting in high rates of political participation as a result. As in Arizona, the state's indigenous population has been assigned a number of reservations. For the most part, intergroup violence has largely been confined to whites, Native Americans, and Hispanics and has remained largely sporadic but significant nevertheless. In this case also, Native American rights were granted relatively early in the state's history and this minority has experienced increasing independence over time while later immigrant minorities have maintained their social organization to significant degrees. Again, the situation reflects medium rather than high levels of colonialism when compared to other states in the country, as we shall see. The state's demographic composition, minority social organization, and medium levels of conflict tend to exhibit its particular history.

Nevada was likewise dominated by Spain and Mexico earlier in its history and was ceded to the United States by treaty in 1848 (Beatty and Beatty 1976). A number of mining strikes occurred. The indigenous population was assigned a number of reservations, while the legislature attempted to exclude Chinese labor and immigration towards the end of the nineteenth century. Hispanics remain a significant proportion of the state's current population. As is well known, the state was the site of a large number of nuclear tests in the 1950's. With its predominantly white majority, the area has not experienced high levels of intergroup conflict; nevertheless, conservative racial reactions and labor issues reflect the powerful effects of limited colonialism in this case.

Texas, also dominated by Spain and Mexico, was once part of both these countries. In 1848 Mexico relinquished all claims to the area after being defeated during the Texas Revolution (Fehrenbach 1968). The state was later involved in the Civil War and affected by the Spanish-American War. The area's population contains significant numbers of Hispanics, particularly Mexican Americans, and black slave descendants. The former have been subject to 'conflict' based colonialism (Moore, 1970), resulting in limited levels of political activity among this minority. While the state has been affected by a number of wars historically, its general level of intergroup conflict has been generally medium rather than extreme; however, a recent lynch-like torture and murder of an African American by white extremists has highlighted the area's tradition of racial violence. While this case generally fits the general category assigned to it, Texas also contains negative features typical of more colonial settings: its history of border conflict and frontier violence continue to be reflected in its current problems of immigration control, migrant labor, refugee issues, and minority poverty. Founded on international conflict, and subject to continuing immigration problems, the state is far from harmonious, revealed in its relatively violent history. Future events, no doubt, will continue to reflect the state's problematic background.

California was also subject to the claims of adjacent and more distant societies: Spain, Great Britain, and Mexico were most prominently involved. Significant conflict with the indigenous population occurred, many of whom were confined to reservations. The 1840's gold rush had a significant demographic impact on the state (Beck and Williams 1972). While slavery was abolished during the same decade and California became a free state soon after, significant urban race riots and protests occurred in later decades, with the 1990's known for its reversal of affirmative action policies. While famous for the nontraditional lifestyles and protests of the 1960's, the state has experienced significant levels of intergroup violence and inequality, particularly during recent decades. Its population, like others in this category, is diverse, including large groups of Hispanics, Blacks, and Asians. Subject to 'economic' colonialism (Moore 1970), Mexican Americans in this state have experienced inconsistent immigration policies over the decades, resulting in very low levels of political activity among this group. The state's history of diverse immigration has no doubt contributed to the evolution of a highly complex socioeconomic situation, with stark contrasts in wealth and poverty, ethnic pluralism, minority protests, and white conservative backlash. Once known for its "tolerant lifestyle," the region has developed a new reputation for racial violence, criminal notoriety, and white conservatism. Given its colonial foundation, complex patterns of immigration, and political dynamics, this may not be surprising. Clearly, the state's historical attraction of significant numbers of new residents has declined in the face of economic and political change.

We turn finally to Colorado, an area also subject to Mexican control, ceded to the United States in 1848. Intergroup conflict involved whites and Native Americans, miner strikes, Japanese relocation, the political influence of the KKK, and long-term resistance to school racial integration, particularly during the 1970's. Again, its population is diverse, with significant proportions of Mexicans and blacks (May 1987). With its past history of white-Native American conflict, conservative racial movements, and resistance to integration, the region reveals significant, if limited, features of the colonial process, a result, perhaps, of its early types of intergroup contact, migration patterns, demographic changes, and resultant social relations. This case emphasizes the potent, if limited, effects of medium levels of colonialism on intergroup relations.

Examining these states together, they generally involve external control and eventual cession, significant conflict with indigenous groups and their assignment to reservations, creation of racially and ethnically diverse populations, sporadic intergroup violence over time, high economic development through a variety of activities, emergence of cultural pluralism particularly with regard to religion, eventual shift from external to colonial control reflecting *limited* colonial independence, and medium levels of intergroup violence focusing on the establishment of dominance, indigenous control, and later racial competition. These kinds of situation tend to reflect *limited levels* of *colonialism,* mediated by migrant elite competition with adjacent powers, early contact with initially powerful indigenous populations, and the *later* immigration of other minorities in the industrial-urban context. These types of situation tend to produce *medium* degrees of intergroup *conflict*. Again, this is *not* to argue that significant levels of violence or intergroup inequality are largely absent; rather, when conditions limited the colonial process to external migration, less exploitive and destructive group relations tend to result. These characteristics are summarized in Table 6.2., underscoring their subjection to external influence, demographic diversity, somewhat negative ecological frontiers, highly developed and diverse economies, and medium levels of intergroup conflict, including racial and labor strife.

Conclusions

In this chapter we have focused on states subject to lower levels and degrees of colonial formation, including more isolated and less accessible regions of the country as well as those initially controlled by neighboring powers. The former reflected progressive rather than sudden colonial dominance, demographic heterogeneity, generally positive historical frontiers, strong economies, and relatively low levels of intergroup conflict. The latter, on the other hand, revealed their subjection to external powers, demographic diversity, somewhat negative ecological frontiers, largely agricultural and mining-based economies, and medium levels of intergroup conflict such as racial and labor strife. Both situational types tend to reflect limited types of colonial domination and somewhat positive ecological frontiers, combined with demographic diversity and strong economies, resulting in limited to medium levels of intergroup conflict. Clearly, less colonial situations tend to be somewhat lower in their general levels of social violence. In chapter 7 we turn to states formed through higher levels of colonialism with more negative social consequences as a result.

Table 6.2 Limited Colonialism: The Impact of Adjacent Societies

Cases	Historical	Demographic	Ecological	Economic	Sociocultural	Political	Psychological
Arizona	Part of Mexico, Indian conflict	High diversity	Medium intergroup conflict	High economic development	High diversity	Control, cession	Medium intergroup conflict
New Mexico	Part of Mexico, Indian conflict	High diversity	Sporadic conflict	High economic development	High diversity	Control, cession	Medium intergroup conflict
Nevada	Part of Mexico, Indian conflict	High diversity	Limited racial and labor conflict	High economic development	High diversity	Control, cession	Medium intergroup conflict
Texas	Part of Mexico, wars	High diversity	War frontiers	High economic development	High diversity	Control, wars	Medium intergroup conflict
California	External claims	High diversity	Early and later conflict	High economic development	High diversity	Control, cession	Medium intergroup conflict
Colorado	Control, cession	High diversity	Racial and labor strife	High economic development	High diversity	Control, conflict	Medium intergroup conflict

7

Intergroup Relations Within the United States: The More Colonial

In this chapter we move to states subject to higher levels of colonialism: those dominated by invading whites; and the most colonial regions of the country, involving slavery and the highest levels of intergroup conflict. In their case, most, if not all, of the features of colonialism are present, resulting in more problematic kinds of intergroup relations. We begin with states settled and largely dominated by white majorities.

States Dominated by Invading Whites

Many states fall into the category of medium colonialism, consisting of situations which are predominantly white in population, indicating relatively high levels of ethnic diversity, with limited numbers of minorities. Historically, they have been subject to migration, subordination, and immigration, revealing moderate levels and types of intergroup conflict, including racial, religious, and economic strife. They have also experienced more positive intergroup developments such as the abolition of slavery and implementation of minority civil rights. Virtually every case, however, is founded on high levels of initial white-Native American violence.

A number are largely restricted to early conflict between the indigenous population and invading whites from a number of European countries. Nebraska, New Hampshire, North Dakota, New Jersey, South Dakota, and Wisconsin tend to fall into this group.

The first of these experienced invading Spanish, French and U.S. explorers, resulting in very high levels of white-Indian violence, land cession, establishment of reservations, and continuing indigenous resistance (Olson 1966). The destructive effect of colonial subordination of an indigenous population is clearly illustrated in this case, with continuing consequences. New Hampshire was subjected to the negative effects of incoming British and French explorers, resulting in Indian wars and long-term conflict with these original settlers (Squires 1956). In this case, conflict was religious, racial, and international, again highlighting the destructive consequences of external colonial immigration. While limited in the range of minorities involved, the state experienced significant levels of intergroup conflict nevertheless. New Jersey was dominated by the Dutch and British, resulting eventually in Indian land cessions and reservations also in this state settled predominantly by Europeans (Fleming 1977). While comparatively limited, racial conflict occurred later in this state. North Dakota experienced similar European incursions, particularly of the Scotch and Irish, eventually resulting in Indian land cessions and establishment of reservations (Robinson 1966). South Dakota was subject to French influence in particular, again resulting in land cessions, reservations, and in this case, very long-term conflict with Native Americans, including the 1973 Wounded Knee incident and related law suits (Schell 1975). Finally, Wisconsin represents another case of invading Europeans, particularly Germans in this case, resulting in Indian wars, land cessions, and reservations which varied in size over time (Nesbit 1989). Together these states represent prime examples of the initial stages of colonialism: invasion of an area by external migrant elites who subordinate the indigenous population, expropriate most of their resources, particularly land, segregate them into restricted areas, and become ethnically diverse through immigration but remain largely racially homogeneous and dominant. Consequent minority group conflict has been relatively limited in extent and frequency, often occurring in particular contexts (e.g., urban). As we shall see, the other states in this general category were founded on these processes but experienced more negative intergroup consequences.

Missouri and Utah were also founded on these types of colonial processes but encountered the immigration of significant

numbers of Mormons, resulting in high levels of religious conflict on occasion. The former involved conflict with Native
Americans and their eventual removal from the state, experienced a war between Mormons and others in 1838, war over
slavery later that century, an automobile industry strike in the
1930's, and largely conflict-free school desegregation in the
1950's and 1970's (Meyer 1970). Thus, Missouri's history involved colonial racial, ethnic, and labor conflict in a state pre-
dominately white in population. Utah, as is well-known, was
also embroiled in long-term nineteenth century conflict with
Mormons over their doctrine and practices, particularly
polygamy (May 1987). The state also established Indian reservations and is racially, ethnically, and religiously relatively homogeneous. Accordingly, colonial situations which involve the immigration of ethnic groups significantly different in culture from
the dominant elite tend to experience religious conflict, occasionally at destructive levels, and segregate indigenous populations under very controlled conditions. While limited in other
forms of intergroup strife, they have nevertheless experienced
other problems created by their colonial backgrounds.

Other states, again founded on colonial processes, also reacted
against incoming minorities, particularly when they felt threat-
ened by them economically. Oregon, for example, reacted against
its Chinese and Japanese residents by excluding them from land-
ownership. They also excluded free blacks from the state in the
nineteenth-century and earlier established reservations for Native
Americans (Dicken 1979). Washington was the site of anti-Chinese
riots in 1885 and later passed a law excluding Chinese and Japanese residents from land-ownership. A large number of the latter
were later transferred to relocation camps during World War II
(Avery 1967). Continuing state battles over Indian fishing rights
also reflect poorly on the state's general race relations. Wyoming's
history was marred by early conflict with Native Americans, the
1885 mob killing of Chinese coal miners, and later World War II establishment of a Japanese relocation center (Mead 1982). Clearly,
these states not only subordinated and segregated the indigenous
population; they also opposed the economic and political threat
posed by incoming racial minorities and treated them very negatively also. From this it is clear that colonial elites act to protect

their interests in a number of ways, including minority exclusion and discrimination, when deemed necessary.

Some states in this category, while abolishing slavery, also experienced later levels of racial violence. Connecticut and New Jersey, for example, were the scenes of dramatic urban riots in the 1960's (Andersen 1975; Fleming 1977). The former involved early subordination of Native Americans and post–World War II immigration of African Americans, while the latter also experienced urban black settlement. Conflict over desegregation occurred in Kentucky during the 1970's, a state which subordinated Native Americans and later excluded slaves from the area (Hall 1979), while the 1980's saw the police bombing of black radicals in Philadelphia, Pennsylvania, a state which also excluded slaves and later experienced labor and racial violence (Channing 1977). Thus, while these states tended to be racially homogeneous, they were still subject to significant outbreaks of racial violence involving immigrant minorities.

Other regions, such as Delaware, Idaho, Minnesota, Montana, and West Virginia have experienced significant labor conflict, including strikes, repeated labor violence, and in some cases, antiunion legislation. The first of these was founded in the face of significant Indian resistance (Hoffecker 1977), while Idaho experienced Indian uprisings, established reservations for them, and also built a Japanese internment camp during the 1940's (Peterson 1976). Minnesota was also founded on high levels of Native American violence and expelled some of them from the state (Blegen 1975). Montana was the scene of army massacres of Native Americans and continuing labor conflict during this century (Farr & Toole 1978). West Virginia experienced Indian wars and attacks along with a number of twentieth century labor conflict (Rice 1985). While these states all experienced colonial foundation and associated violence with the indigenous population, strife in the shipping, mining, and trucking industries has also been particularly evident in these situations, highlighting the salience of class and related issues in the economic sphere. Colonial situations, regardless of minority diversity, involve significant levels of elite economic interests and exploitation, resulting in their conservative, protectionist behavior in the face of potential competition.

Taken together, the above contexts generally reflect the colonial processes of migration, subordination, and limited immigration, involving populations which are largely racially homogeneous. While *medium* in their *colonial* characteristics, they have experienced significant levels of conflict involving Native, Asian, and African Americans, religious minorities and labor sectors on *occasion.* However, this is *not* to imply they have lacked positive intergroup relations entirely: a number of these states abolished slavery early and facilitated racial and gender-based civil rights. Connecticut, Kentucky, New York and Pennsylvania, for example, while similarly founded on colonial migration and indigenous subordination, were anti-slavery early in their history and, in some cases, excluded slaves entirely from their regions of the country (Andersen 1975; Channing 1977; Kammen 1975; Cochran 1978). As indicated above, however, this did *not* mean they avoided later racial violence such as urban riots.

Some regions also organized movements and passed laws directed against slavery. These occurred in Kansas, Maine, Massachusetts, Rhode Island, and Vermont. The first of these, while founded on the subordination of Native Americans, prohibited slavery in the 1850's and later experienced a significant in-migration of freed slaves into the area and later reduction in K.K.K. membership (Gaeddert 1974). Maine, while containing Indian reservations and a history of their dominance, has a history of anti-slavery activity and later settlement of Indian land suits (Berchen 1973). Massachusetts is also well-known for its revolutionary and anti-slavery tradition, marred later by Boston busing conflict (Brown 1978). Rhode Island remains distinctive for its early abolition of slavery and strong church/state separation tradition (McLoughlin 1978). Finally, Vermont was one of the earliest states to oppose slavery and ratify the anti-slavery amendment (Morrissery 1981).

Other states, specifically Iowa, Missouri, New York, Oklahoma, and Oregon, actively facilitated minority civil rights. Black civil rights were established early in Iowa's history despite its history of Indian conflict and exclusion (Sage 1987). Equal education for African Americans was legislated in Oklahoma in 1948, a state which experienced Indian immigration and their early organization (Morgan & Morgan 1977), while racial equality in housing and salaries began in Oregon in the 1950's (Dicken & Dicken 1979). Women were granted the franchise in New York in 1917, a state which also abolished slavery earlier (Kammen 1975), as they were in Oregon in 1912, while school desegregation in Missouri began largely peacefully in the 1950's (Meyer 1970). While all these states were colonially founded and many of them experienced significant levels of racial, ethnic, religious, and economic violence, some of them rejected slavery early in their history and established minority civil rights well in advance of many others.

Viewing these states as a whole, they generally involve external migration, control, and eventually cession, high rates of violence with indigenous groups, relatively homogeneous racial populations, ethnic diversity, high levels of economic development including specialization, early establishment of colonial dominance, and medium levels of racial, ethnic, and economic conflict. On the more positive side, many of these states abolished slavery and implemented minority civil rights comparatively early in their histories. These kinds of situation tend to reflect *medium* levels of *colonialism*, based on migrant elite subordination of indigenous populations, control of their resources, their segregation in reservations, and ongoing economic development of these regions. Under conditions of racial dominance and relative homogeneity, racial, ethnic, and economic conflict has occurred, sometimes in violent ways, but largely sporadic and balanced by attempts to implement minority civil rights, at least in some cases. Here conditions of *medium colonialism* tend to result in *limited* degrees and types of intergroup *conflict*, balanced in some cases by attempts to ensure minority civil rights. While significant levels and types of intergroup violence are present, they tend to be more sporadic and less destructive. These characteristics are summarized in Table 7.1, underscoring their white dominance, control and cession foundations, negative ecological frontiers, economic variation, and wide variety of intergroup conflict, including racial, religious, and labor-related types. The generally negative consequences of white migration and dominance are clear in these trends.

The Most Colonial States

The most colonial states are based on colonial migration, subordination, and forcible importation of minorities, in many cases for labor purposes. Consequent intergroup conflict tends to be high and violent. While slavery is not present in every situation, these regions contain significant populations of African Americans, often in urban contexts. However, in each case intergroup violence is present either in the form of white opposition to black rights or race riots. Most of these situations are located in the American South and Midwest. They highlight the long-term and over-whelmingly destructive effects of high levels of colonialism, in-volving the creation, segregation, exploitation, and dominance of minority groups in a rigid, largely caste-like manner. Consequent intergroup relations are inevitably conflict-ridden and resistant to positive change.

These states were all founded on white subordination of Native Americans, Expropriation of their land, and in many cases, the forcible importation of African American slaves. Southern states, furthermore, were often founded by an ethnically homogeneous elite, particularly white Protestants, with other ethnic groups mi-grating into these areas later. Many contemporary black are de-scendants of earlier slaves. Some of them have experienced white extremist reactions to Reconstruction, particularly in the form of the K.K.K., while other have been subject to attempts by white mil-itants to restrict black voting and school integration rights. Inter-group relations in most of them have been very negative, includ-ing black riots and white violent resistance to minority integration. These states tend to be the most negative and violence-prone of all, given their highly colonial foundation.

A number of southern and mid-western regions experienced K.K.K. and related racial violence. These included Arkansas, Flor-ida, Georgia, and Indiana. While slavery was abolished during 1864 in Arkansas, discriminatory laws, racial KKK-related vio-lence, Jim Crow policies, poll taxes, voting restrictions, and the battle over educational integration marred the state's later history considerably (Ashmore 1978). Removal of both Native and African Americans was attempted earlier in this extremely nega-tive colonial context. Florida is also known for its history of In-dian wars, slavery, lynching, K.K.K. violence, religious conser-vatism, racial police incidents, race riots, and refugee situations (Jahoda 1976). While a tourist haven, the state clearly does not represent the land of racial harmony. Georgia has a particularly conflict-ridden background, including military rule, slavery, overt

Table 7.1 Medium Colonialism: Dominant Whites

Cases	Historical	Demographic	Ecological	Economic	Sociocultural	Political	Psychological
States with White-Indian conflict	Control, cession	Few minorities	Indian conflict	High economic development	High diversity	Cession, control	Indian wars
States with religious conflict	Control, Mormons	Some minorities	Religious conflict	High economic development	High diversity	Religious control	Religious conflict
States with Asian conflict	Control, cession	Some minorities	Racial conflict	High economic development	Low diversity	Cession, control	Asian conflict
States with Black conflict	Control, cession	Some minorities	Limited racial conflict	High economic development	Low diversity	Cession, control	Black conflict
States with labor conflict	Control, cession	Few minorities	Limited labor conflict	High economic development	Low diversity	Cession, control	Labor conflict
Slavery abolition states	Control, cession	Some miorities	Limited racial conflict	High economic development	Low diversity	Cession, control	Slavery abolition
States with high civil rights	Control, cession	Few minorities	Limited racial conflict	High economic development	Low diversity	Cession, control	High civil rights

rejection of Reconstruction, high levels of K.K.K. activity, violent white defense of segregation, and destructive race riots (Coleman 1978). Finally, Indiana, while somewhat lower in racial conflict than these other areas, experienced significant conflict with Native Americans who were eventually expelled, rejected black settlers in the 1850's, and recruited hundreds of thousands of K.K.K. members by the 1920's (Peckham 1978). Clearly, in these areas of the country, whites responded to racial change in extremist ways, resisting them violently in many cases, reflecting the highly colonial nature of these regions of the country.

White militancy also occurred in Louisiana, Ohio, South Carolina, and Virginia. In the first of these, the White League repressed a black rebellion during the 1870's, while blacks were disenfranchised twenty years later, interracial athletics were banned in the 1960's, schools were closed rather than desegregated during the 1950's, and anti-integration riots took place the following decade (Davis 1969). Ironically, while black civil rights were established early by the state, whites later acted against their enforcement in a very destructive manner. Ohio, while less conflict-prone, experienced significant levels of Indian-white conflict during its founding history, passed laws in the early 1800's to restrict black rights and movement, by the 1840's the state contained no more Native Americans, and more recent decades have seen labor strikes (Roseboom & Weisenburger 1969). African Americans in South Carolina were subject to slavery, the intimidation of white militants in the 1870's, disenfranchisement in the 1890's, upholding of segregation in the 1950's, continuing discrimination the next decade, and white riots against busing during the 1970's (Lander & Ackerman 1973). Finally, Virginia's past is notorious for its history of indentured servitude, support of slavery, Jim Crow laws, constitutional support of educational segregation, official opposition to integration, and school closings to avoid desegregation (Rubin 1977). Militant white opposition to legitimate racial change in these areas of the country is notable and extreme in these cases, clearly reflecting their colonial features, *viz.*, colonial elite, indigenous subordination, forcible importation of minorities for labor purposes, and violent attempts to maintain their exploitive, subordinate status. Intergroup violence in their case tends to reflect white interests in a traditionally caste-type context.

A third group of states experienced high levels of black violence against white racism and white opposition to integration. These included Alabama, Illinois, Maryland, Michigan, Mississippi, North Carolina, and Tennessee. The first of these has a remarkable history of racial exploitation and violence, including slavery, the 1931 Scottsboro Trial, 1950's civil rights black activism, white harassment and opposition epitomized in the views of George Wallace, and high levels of racial conflict generally (Hamilton 1977). Alabama reflects a past of multiple claims and invasions, Indian conflict and removal, black slavery, high numbers of racial incidents and violence, and significant black militancy- all the major elements of the typical colonial situation. Illinois has a violent past also, including black exclusion in the 1850's, the 1917 East St. Louis race riots, 1919 Chicago violence, 1968 urban riots, and 1969 Black Panther trial (Bridges & Davis 1984). Conflict with the indigenous population, slavery, and racial violence are all part of this particular situation. Maryland, with its history of religious conflict, black servitude, and labor conflict, was the scene of anti-segregation demonstrations and riots following Martin Luther King's assassination during the 1960's (Bode 1978). Michigan, subject to French, British, and Spanish influence, and the scene of significant black urban migration also experienced auto strikes as well as race riots in Detroit, both in 1943 and 1967 (Santer 1977). Mississippi, one of the country's poorest and most colonial states, has a long tradition of racial violence, including the 1874 Vicksburg riots, maintenance of segregation, brutal resistance to civil rights workers, negative reaction to racial demonstrations, and integration-related turbulence (McLemore 1973). Despite recent improvements, this part of the nation remains one of the most dismal economically and socially. North Carolina, the scene of Indian and religious wars, disenfranchised blacks in the 1830's and was the scene of anti-segregation opposition and related violence during the 1960's and 1970's (Powell 1977). One of the most politically conservative, the state has far to go in significantly improving its race relations. Finally, anti-desegregation hostility and pro-integration demonstrations occurred in Tennessee during the 1950's and 1960's, with Martin Luther King assassinated in Memphis in 1968 (Corlew 1981). Founded on Indian wars and French cessions, its negative history includes black dis-enfranchisement, Indian removals, creationist teaching, and anti-integrationist riots. Again, all the central features of the colonial situation are present: external migration, indigenous subordination, resource expropriation, forcible importation of minorities, and violent resistance to racial change. In such a context, violence is symptomatic of colonial dominance and exploitation, as well as minority rejection of their subordination.

Taken together, these states represent *high levels of colonialism*, given their experience of external migration, subordination of indigenous populations, and forcible importation of minorities for labor purposes. Demographically they are relatively homogeneous, containing large white and black populations with the former often ethnically limited, and reveal histories of racial violence involving white resistance to black advancement and the latter's negative reaction to racial dominance, discrimination, and segregation. Some states were subject to the activities of the KKK, with others experiencing other forms of white militancy. Others experienced less formally organized types of racial violence but highly destructive nevertheless. Clearly, these types of *social contexts* tend to be the most *conflict-prone*, given their *historical formation:* situations subject to external migration, subordination, and involuntary importation produce the most *caste-like* exploitive arrangements, in which elite interests drive attempts to *maintain* their control of the society and *resist* minority attempts to change it. Subordinate groups, in turn, *react against* such dominance, resulting in inevitable *intergroup conflict*. Consequently, these types of situations tend to be the most negative at *all* social levels—individual, group, and institutional. High levels of colonialism inevitably result in significant types and degrees of intergroup conflict. These characteristics are summarized in Table 7.2, emphasizing their extremist backgrounds, heavy use of slavery, significant black populations, economic diversity, and high levels of racial violence, reflected in white resistance to attempted change. Clearly, the most colonial states tend to be the most conflict-ridden.

Conclusions

This chapter has focused on the country's more heavily colonized states. We found that those dominated by invading whites revealed their white homogeneity, external control and cession

Table 7.2 High Colonialism: Migration, Subordination, and Forcible Importation

Cases	Historical	Demographic	Ecological	Economic	Sociocultural	Political	Psychological
White extremist states	Cession, slavery	High racial division	High racial conflict	High economic development	Low diversity	Control, cession	High psychological racial violence
White militancy states	Cession, slavery	High racial division	High racial conflict	High economic development	Low diversity	Control, cession	High psychological racial violence
Racially violent states	Cession, slavery	High racial division	High racial conflict	High economic development	Low diversity	Control, cession	High psychological racial violence

foundations, negative ecological frontiers, economic diversity, and wide variety of intergroup conflict, including racial, religious, and labor-related strife. The most colonial states, on the other hand, indicated extremist backgrounds, heavy use of slavery, significant black populations, economic diversity, and high levels of racial violence, particularly reflected in white resistance to attempted social change. According to these trends, it appears reasonable to conclude that high levels of colonialism tend to result in the most negative and destructive types of intergroup relations, particularly as indicated in elite resistance and racial violence.

We turn to examine the society as a whole.

8

Intergroup Relations Within the United States as a Whole

We have divided this society into a number of specific *contact situations:* (1) isolated and less colonial states: (2) states initially controlled by adjacent powers; (3) those dominated by invading whites; and, (4) the most colonial, involving slavery and high levels of racial conflict. Essentially, these situational types may be arranged along a *colonial continuum,* ranging from low to high colonialism and associated levels of intergroup conflict. This view is based on the notion that the more features of the colonial process are present in a particular context, the more conflict-ridden intergroup relations within them tend to be.

We drew a number of major conclusions as follows:

1. the first type of state context involved gradual external domination, demographic diversity, an economy which included tourism, sociocultural heterogeneity, limited external control, and relatively low levels of intergroup conflict (i.e., Alaska, Hawaii, Puerto Rico). We emphasized that they were founded generally on comparatively limited types of external migration, control, and domination, resulting in limited types and levels of intergroup violence;;

2. states subject to the influence of adjacent societies were often originally part of Mexico, resulting in relatively large Hispanic populations. Some situations also attracted fairly high numbers of blacks. Intergroup conflict in these situations tended to be limited and somewhat sporadic in frequency. They have largely been the scene of violence against Native

Americans, the creation of reservations for them, and the immigration of African Americans in some cases, particularly
Colorado and California, with the latter experiencing race
riots, significant white violence, and recent reversal of affirmative action policies. These states included Arizona, California, Colorado, New Mexico, Nevada, and Texas;

3. states subject to the dominance of invading whites tend to reflect racial dominance and relatively demographic homogeneity, resulting in medium levels of racial, ethnic, and economic conflict, occasionally violent, but largely sporadic and
balanced in some cases by attempts to ensure minority rights.
Examples include Nebraska, New Hampshire, New Jersey,
Wisconsin, Missouri, Utah, Oregon, Wyoming, Delaware,
Montana, West Virginia, Kansas, Rhode Island, and Vermont.
Historically, these regions have been subject to migration,
subordination, and immigration, revealing moderate levels
of intergroup strife and attempts, in some cases, to abolish
slavery and implement minority civil rights;

4. fourthly, states founded on migration, subordination, and
forcible importation of minorities represent the highest levels of colonialism, involving relative racial and ethnic homogeneity in many cases, high economic diversity, and the
most extreme levels and types of intergroup violence. Most
of these states are located in the South and Midwest, and
include Arkansas, Florida, Georgia, Indiana, Louisiana,
Ohio, South Carolina, Virginia, Alabama, Illinois, Maryland, Michigan, Mississippi, North Carolina, and Tennessee. While slavery was not present in every case, these
states contain significant populations of African Americans, particularly in urban contexts, with intergroup violence expressed in the form of white opposition to black
rights or race riots. As the most colonial-type states, these
have tended to be the most violent.

Examining these four situations together, they range from limited colonialism, through medium levels, to the highest types of
external exploitation. Levels of intergroup conflict also vary from
low and limited, through medium, to very high, both in type and
degree. From this it is clear that the society, while colonial as a

whole, varies significantly in its *internal* levels and types of colonialism: those less accessible and/or subject to all the major elements of colonialism (*viz.*, external migration, subordination, expropriation, importation, and exploitation) are significantly less likely to experience high levels of intergroup conflict at every level within it and vice versa. These levels or types of colonialism within the U.S. are summarized in Table 8.1. Each type clearly varies with respect to its historical, demographic, ecological, economic, sociocultural, political, and psychological features. Examining each column, they vary from gradual dominance to cession and slavery, high indigenous populations to predominantly migrants, particularly whites and blacks, limited to high levels of intergroup conflict, varying types of economies, high to relatively low demographic diversity, limited to high dominance, and low to high levels of racial conflict. States lower in colonial foundation tend to reflect limited types of external and internal dominance, higher indigenous populations, and low to medium levels of intergroup conflict. However, situations subject to higher levels of outside dominance and exploitation tend to be more homogeneous demographically, involve slavery in some cases, and experience a variety of conflict types, including the most destructive racial kind. According to these trends, the higher a state's level of colonialism, the more migrant their populations, and the more negative and violent their intergroup relations tend to be. While such a trend does *not* operate in any kind of simplistic, uniform manner, subject to variations produced by subsequent migrations and related events, this proposition appears to hold consistently, for the most part. In any event, this approach highlights the need to understand intergroup relations at state and regional levels in terms of their historical foundation and subsequent dynamics, ranging, in this case, from low to high levels of external exploitation or colonialism.

We turn to discuss some general conclusions of this analysis, based on this underlying colonial continuum.

Conclusions: The Colonial Continuum

This part of our analysis has highlighted America's colonial context, specifically the general processes involved in its foundation, elite values, institutionalized inequality, negative historical fron-

Table 8.1 Types of Colonialism within the United States

Cases	Historical	Demographic	Ecological	Economic	Sociocultural	Political	Psychological
Isolated states	Gradual dominance	Few minorities	Limited conflict	High economic development	High diversity	Limited dominance	Relatively low intergroup conflict
Adjacent states	Initial external control, part of Mexico	Few minorities	Limited, sporadic conflict	High economic development	High diversity	Limited dominance	Medium intergroup conflict
Invading whites	Control, cession	Some minorities	Limited racial, labor conflict	High economic development	High/Low diversity	Control, cession	Medium racial, religious, labor conflict and civil rights
Most colonial states	Cession, slavery	High racial division	High racial conflict	High economic development	Low diversity	Control, cession	High psychological racial violence

tiers, and continuity of negative intergroup contact. We also indicated that American intergroup relations occur within an integrated hierarchy defining individual social status, reflecting elite interests and ideologies, and subject to social change but in a conservative manner over time. Finally, we placed intergroup relations at the state level along a colonial continuum, ranging from the least to highest types of colonialism. At this point of our analysis, it is appropriate to outline this continuum as a whole and draw some general conclusions from it. This continuum particularly highlights a state's location, extent of colonialism, and consequent types of intergroup relations. Table 8.2 outlines the major characteristics of this continuum, as applied to the four types of states. As can be seen, colonialism ranges from low, involving more isolated situations with positive intergroup relations, limited adjacent contexts which include limited violence, medium situations dominated by whites, again experiencing limited intergroup conflict, and the most colonial, including slavery, and resulting in very negative social consequences.

The above typology also highlights a number of specific conclusions as follows:

1. colonialism is a matter of *degree* rather than categorical distinction, i.e., *all* U.S. states involve a number of colonial features and most of them reveal problematic intergroup relations of *some* kind, with consequent violence to a limited degree, no matter how generally positive they may be. While they vary along this continuum, then, they are *all* colonial to *some* degree;

2. consequently, they may all be viewed as *particular* societal *contexts*, more or less potentially conflict-ridden, rather than fixed, absolute categories. They are consequently subject to significant social change, effected by processes such as migration, economic development, and political events;

3. furthermore, while subject to categorization, they all possess relatively *unique* histories and features, making their intergroup relations less than entirely predictable. Thus, particular kinds of stress might result in violence in otherwise apparently peaceful contexts, but not generally long-term in nature; alternatively, contexts typically violent do not *always*

Table 8.2 The Colonial Continuum

Colonialism Levels	Location		Foundation				Intergroup Relations	
	Isolated	Adjacent	Migr.	Subordinate	Import.	Slavery	Positive	Negative
Low	+	−	+	+	+	−	+	−
Limited	−	+	+	+	+	−	+	+
Medium	−	−	+	+	+	−	+	+
High	−	−	+	+	+	+	−	+

operate in such a fashion, subject to particular combinations of events and social reactions;

4. while as states they may be conceptualized as part of general regions or areas of the society, as such they represent self-maintaining political, economic, and cultural units. The 'state' notion thus retains empirical significance, given their particular histories, identities, patterns of settlement, and relatively unique state-wide institutions;

5. taken as a whole, these units demonstrate that competition and conflict are part of *all* social situations, regardless of particular type, although varying in type, dynamics, and intergroup consequences. Clearly, *all* contexts in which groups come into contact with one another, regardless of how positive they might be, involve competition and therefore potential conflict of some kind, no matter how limited. Differences among 'types' may thus be more 'apparent' than 'real;'

6. however, some contexts appear *relatively* more *flexible* and *harmonious* than others. Hawaii, for example, is clearly more generally harmonious than a state like Mississippi, with its history of violence, poverty, and discrimination. Again, however, both situations involve intergroup competition and potential violence of some kind no matter how limited. Nevertheless, as contexts they are distinctively different with regard to likely degrees and kinds of conflict ;

7. from a policy perspective, understanding differing contexts and their *conflict potential* becomes crucial to effecting positive change within them. Such insight is based both on typological characteristics and relatively unique traits at the state level; finally,

8. the typology underlines the relevance of any society's *ecological location* and *societal foundation* to understanding its *subsequent intergroup relations*. Clearly, those relations reflect a context's particular environment, social formation, and intergroup dynamics within it. Understanding a society's relative access, formative intergroup sequences, and general dynamics become crucial to appreciating its internal social relations. On the national level, however, political policies are forced to cover a range of contextual types, despite their relatively unique characteristics. While some adjustments

might be feasible, limits regarding 'tailor-made' policy implementation clearly exist in matters of national policy. The battle between federal policy and state needs will continue, whatever allowances are made for 'local' reactions.

Having studied colonialism and its varieties within one particular society, we turn to examine intergroup relations on a worldwide basis, focusing on similar factors.

PART THREE

Intergroup Relations Worldwide

9

Intergroup Relations Worldwide: Isolated and Traditional Societies

Our central focus in this project is on the kinds of contact situations behind the formation of particular societal contexts which define the kinds of social interaction which take place within them, varying in their levels of colonialism or negative migrant/indigenous contact. We have explored these factors and their varying impact within a particular society, highlighting different kinds of formative contact situations, ranging from low to high colonialism; this section of our analysis applies this perspective to an analysis of intergroup relations on a worldwide basis, ranging from low to high levels of colonialism and differentiated by general levels of intergroup conflict.

Six *types* of *societal context* will be examined by conflict level: (1) those located in *isolated* and *remote areas*, less accessible to external domination and exploitation (who largely experienced low levels of intergroup conflict); (2) *traditional societies*, originally ruled by monarchies or other types of dynasty, subject to significant types of social change over time (both low and high conflict); (3) countries subjected to *external control and/or cession*, with varying societal consequences (low and high conflict); (4) societies exposed to high levels of *outside invasion*, with diverse patterns of consequent intergroup relations (low and high conflict); (5) areas which became *protectorates*, subject to external sponsorship or exploitation (low and high conflict); and, (6) situations formed predominantly through external *colonialism*, differing in their levels of ensuing societal violence (high and low conflict). Again, such a typology is based on the nature and predominant type of societal formation, ranging from low colonialism/high independence to the opposite situation.

We begin with the first of these: isolated, remote areas which generally experience relatively low conflict levels. Given their limited access to outsiders, they have not generally been subject to the kinds of external domination and exploitation others have often experienced. Consequently, intergroup has tended to occur less often and with less destructive results.

Isolated, Remote Societies

These countries, many of them islands, exist in remote areas and have generally experienced low levels of intergroup conflict. This is *not* to suggest that their location is causal; some such situations are highly conflict-prone, as we shall see. However, in their case, this kind of geographical situation has contributed to the type of contact sequences they have been subject to. These largely consist of the following: islands settled by refugees in which high levels of majority political development occurred; island plantations with similarly positive political experiences; islands governed by external trusts or mandates with little internal violence and high levels of self-government; remote areas in which rural democratization occurred; and colonies in which settler numbers and economic power eventually declined severely, with corollary levels of indigenous political development.

The Bahamas, Barbados, and Iceland involved settlement by external refugees, who developed plantations in some cases, but within which significant levels of democratization took place. The first of these reveals a past in which the original island inhabitants were removed by the Spanish, the area was colonized in the seventeenth century by the British, loyalist refugees settled the area, brought in slaves, and the country experienced gradual but significant democratization until the locals reluctantly accepted independence from Great Britain in 1973. These islands are remarkable for their gradual democratization and movement towards full independence (Albury 1975). Barbados reflects a similar history: Spanish removal of local Indians, British loyalist refugee plantation settlements and slaves, importation of indentured servants, early abolition of slavery, and gradual evolution toward full democracy and independence in 1966. This society is unusual also in its moderate increase in self-government (Greenfield 1966). Of the three, Iceland is perhaps the most unique: founded by refugees from Norway with their slaves from Ireland, the settlers, with their chiefs, formed one of the world's earliest democracies, maximizing local autonomy. While subject to Danish rule for a short period, the country has been fully independent since 1918 and remains one of the most equalitarian and harmonious societies in the world. This island nation is particularly known for its ancient history, ethnic homogeneity, democratic tradition, and almost total lack of intergroup conflict at any point in its history (Hjalmersson 1993). These cases highlight the manner in which *refugee settlement* of *isolated areas*, despite involving colonial situations and types of economic development, may result in high levels of *democratization*.

A number of other island plantations also experienced positive political development. These included Saint Lucia, Saint Vincent and Grenadines, and the Seychelles. The first of these saw the original Arawaks exterminated by the Caribs, after which the country was subject to Spanish, British, and French rule, with Great Britain finally in control during the nineteenth century. Economic activities included sugar plantations and subsistence agriculture. Saint Lucia became self-governing in 1924, implemented a universal franchise in 1951, and finally became independent in 1979. Again, this country is relatively unique in its early self-government and gradual movement towards political independence (Law 1988). Saint Vincent and the Grenadines were also subject to Carib dominance, the influence of the French and British, eventual control by the latter with slavery and plantations, later French invasions, and an eventual truce, resulting in independence in 1979. While the country has experienced a number of disasters and high levels of poverty, it has remained relatively harmonious and generally low in conflict. Its history is remarkable for its early rejection of slavery and tradition of independence (Shephard 1971). The Seychelles were also very isolated, influenced by both French and British, subject to plantations and slavery, and became a crown colony in 1903. Their constitutional development was gradual but continuous and they gained independence in 1976, after which they experienced coups and attempts to impose socialistic arrangements on the area (Franda 1982). While continuing to experience economic limitations, the islands have remained generally free of severe conflict and represent one of Africa's more unique settings, particularly in view of its high levels of miscegenation and gradual movement through home-rule to full independence.

A second set of island plantations, while involving the importation of ethnically diverse labor and related types of conflict, has also remained relatively low in intergroup conflict. This includes Mauritius, Saint Kitts and Nevis, as well as Trinidad and Tobago. The first of these was settled and exploited by the French in the seventeenth century, Britain in the nineteenth century, and was developed using slaves, imported Indian labor, and sugar plantations. While the twentieth century has seen strikes, riots, and fears regarding potential Hindu political dominance, the country has experienced gradual, peaceful, constitutional change, resulting in their independence in 1968. The island's relatively harmonious constitutional development from the 1940's through the 1960's, culminating in eventual independence is particularly remarkable in view of its ethnic pluralism (Bowman 1991). Saint Kitts and Nevis were also subject to French and British control, plantation slavery and imported, indentured Indian labor. They gained independence in 1983, since revealing land, economic, and demographic limitations as well as sugar labor protests (Richardson 1983). However, they have not generally been subject to high rates of intergroup violence. While stratified by class and race, they have remained relatively peaceful nevertheless. Trinidad and Tobago were originally a Spanish possession, surrendered to Britain in 1802. Again, they were subject to plantation development with the use of slave and imported Indian labor, and have experienced labor unrest, political agitation, and even a recent attempted Indian coup (Ryan 1972). However, they have not generally been the scene of high levels of conflict and violence. Their tradition of trade unions, representative councils, and self-government has, perhaps, ensured their relative calm in the face of protest and change. In general, these *island plantations,* while based on colonial exploitation through slavery and imported labor (in some cases), experienced *limited degrees of intergroup conflict* but not at highly destructive, violent levels. For the most part, they reveal constitutional development towards early self-government, democratization and independence. While clearly subject to labor unrest, economic limitations, and ethnic competition, they do not indicate the kinds of violence typical of more colonial situations.

A number of islands became trusts or subject to the mandate of other powers. These include the Marshall Islands, Micronesia, Nauru, Solomon Islands, and Western Samoa. The first of these experienced ineffective Spanish claims in the sixteenth century, nineteenth century German control and later economic development, and WWII Japanese occupation, becoming a U.N. Trust Territory under a U.S. administration in 1947. However, given their isolation and relative homogeneity, these islands have remained largely tranquil. (Hezel 1983). Micronesia has similarly experienced Spanish influence, German economic control, Japanese occupation, and U.N./U.S. trust status, implementing a constitutional government in 1986. Again, they have remained largely peaceful in the face of such external forces (Fluker, Goodman, & Lande 1981). Nauru was also subject to German influence and WWII Japanese occupation, becoming a U.N./Australian Trust in 1947 and achieving independence in 1968. This island reflects continuing Australian influence, phosphate mining activity, and problematic labor and race relations (Viviani 1970). Again, however, large-scale destructive violence was largely absent despite such events. The Solomon Islands encountered French, Spanish, Dutch, and British influence but relatively little external settlement. Nevertheless, kidnaping of potential slaves and indentured workers did take place in the face of local resistance and violence but occurred rarely. Self-government was achieved in 1976 with independence in 1978. The locals' resistance to external domination has no doubt facilitated their freedom (Kent 1973). Finally, Western Samoa, the outcome of an 1899 partition agreement between the U.S. and Germany, experienced British influence also, was subject to gradual political development with European representation, resulting in their 1962 independence. Particularly striking is their political system combining both traditional and modern types of government (McGovern 1988). In these particular cases, *external claims or mandates* resulted in *gradual but steady political development,* with relatively *low levels of intergroup conflict* or *violence.*

Particular kinds of elite and their changing development may also have a major impact on remote areas, as indicated in Costa Rico and Belize. The former country was settled by the Spanish who found the area lacked gold and indigenous labor. As a military elite but unusually democratic in orientation, the Costa Ricans developed a rural democracy, low in feudalism, militarism, and minority indigenous exploitation, and high in democracy and economical development, eventually developing a welfare state (Edelman & Kenen 1989). This society stands out as uniquely developed, low in stratification, and one of the most conflict-free in Central America. Belize, on the other hand, was subjected to the control and exploitation of a very strong British settler elite who monopolized the land and used slaves to develop it. However, economic competition with Great Britain brought slumps and the settler elite's decline; consequently, the black population, while vulnerable to historical exploitation and control, experienced relatively little conflict and achieved independence in 1981. Particularly interesting in this case was the colonial elite's limited economic characteristics and consequent demise in the wake of significant international market changes (Bolland 1977).

The above societies are outlined in Table 9.1 by type of contact and conflict level. It can be seen that these cases suggest that *isolated* or *remote areas settled by external refugees, plantation developers, or unusual elites and/or subject to external trust and/or significant economic decline, tend to experience significant levels of political development and democratization, with relatively low levels of intergroup violence.* This is *not* to assume that the effects of these factors are *causal* in some manner; only to suggest that these kinds of contact situations and consequent ecological developments appear relatively lower in intergroup conflict than many others. As particular societal contexts they have been founded and developed in situations favoring independence rather than colonial domination, resulting in lower levels of intergroup conflict. Their relative isolation and low access to outsiders has reinforced the positive effects of these *particular combinations of circumstances.* As with our earlier analysis of particular regions in the United States, more isolated, remote areas, particularly islands, are often not subject to direct, more complete colonial domination typical of other parts of the world, resulting in more destructive intergroup relations. As we also emphasized, this does *not* imply this is *always* the case: some islands have been subject to exploitive colonial treatment with very negative consequences. What is crucial are the influence of particular

Table 9.1   Isolated, Remote Societies by Country, Type of Contact, and
            Conflict Level

Countries	Type of Contact	Level of Conflict
Bahamas, Barbados, Iceland	Refugee settlement of isolated areas	Low conflict
St. Lucia, St. Vincent and Grenadines, Seychelles	Island plantations who experienced positive political development	Low conflict
Mauritius, St. Kitts and Nevis, Trinidad and Tobago	Island plantations with imported labor	Low conflict
Marshall Islands, Micronesia, Naura, Solomon Islands, Western Samoa	Islands subject to external claims, trusts, or mandates	Low conflict
Costa Rico, Belize	Unusual elites and types of economic development	Low conflict

kinds of factors in specific situations, creating societal contexts favoring or discouraging intergroup violence. We turn to examine conflict levels in traditional societies.

Traditional Societies

These societies include traditional monarchies and dynasties, some of which have experienced comparatively low levels of conflict, others much higher. The former cases tend to involve the following: those who resisted external domination, becoming largely democratic; those attaining internal unity and constitutional monarchies; and those shifting from traditional monarchies to limited political openness.

Norway, San Marino, Belgium, the Netherlands, Austria, and Finland are major examples of the first type. The first of these was originally part of a thirteenth century Scandinavian kingdom under Danish control. The country was eventually ceded to Sweden, declaring its independence in 1905. A modern monarchy was established by plebiscite and the society has experienced a variety of economic, social and political dynamics in recent decades (Eckstein 1966). However, its liberal and democratic traditions, reflecting its founding isolated settlements, fierce independence, and harsh environment, have remained intact, ensuring its relatively conflict-free, independent history. San Marino, an isolated European republic, resisted Italian domination for an extensive period, eventually signed a treaty with the latter in 1862, and has remained a highly equalitarian country with socialist-type policies. Its rejection of external interference and internal elitism makes it a particularly unusual society (Playfair & FitzGibbon 1954). Belgium was originally part of a number of empires, including the Hapsburgs and Netherlands, but revolted in 1830 and became recognized as independent the following year. While its ethnic diversity is reflected in political conflict between the Flemings and Walloons, resulting in a number of relatively unstable governments over time, the country remains a viable democracy in every respect, with a very liberal constitution. It is a prime example of a pluralistic democracy with a history of resistance to outside domination (Reed 1924). The Netherlands were also part of a number of empires, including those developed by Charlemagne, the Hapsburgs, and Napoleon, eventually uniting with Belgium in the nineteenth century. However, they split from the latter in 1830 and eventually became a constitutional monarchy (Goudsblom 1967). With their traditions of fierce independence, regional autonomy, and political liberalism, they remain one of Europe's most viable democracies with little internal conflict; instead, they reveal consistent levels of tolerance and acceptance of outsiders, particularly refugees. Austria is also well-known for its history of domination by external monarchies, including Charlemagne, the Hapsburgs, and Hungary. Experiencing severe defeats in a number of major wars, the country eventually became independent in 1955, with a history largely lacking in internal political violence (Kann 1957). Finally, Finland was subject to seven centuries of Swedish rule and Soviet domination, but eventually negotiated its independence. While experiencing political volatility, the country is a strong parliamentary republic with relatively low levels of intergroup conflict. Despite its history of external domination, the country has demonstrated a remarkable ability to drive out external forces when feasible, negotiate peace treaties when necessary, and maintain its internal political balance (Singleton 1989). Taken as a group, these countries, while originally part of other empires, resisted external dominance, becoming independent democracies with relatively low levels of internal conflict.

A second group eventually achieved internal unity and proceeded to implement constitutional monarchies. Sweden, for example, originally a number of petty kingdoms, was unified with Norway and Denmark in the fourteenth century, eventually revolted against the Danish monarchy, fought wars against a number of European countries, resisted Soviet dominance, and eventually became independent, implementing policies of neutrality, socialism, and a constitutional monarchy. In all of this, the country's ability to maintain its independence in the face of outside aggression is remarkable (Elstob 1979). Denmark, once part of Sweden, Norway, and Iceland, saw the rise and decline of the monarchy, significant constitutional reform, development of middle class liberalism, and increasing local independence. Particularly significant was the development of a royal bureaucracy developed with the help of outsiders, and the country's experience of class-based politics (Miller 1968). Tonga, clearly a very different kind of society, was once an absolute monarchy which underwent civil war and very negative contacts with outsiders, including missionaries, but eventually became a constitutional monarchy under British protection. Its residents fiercely resisted the incursions of outsiders, maintaining their independence effectively over time (Rutherford 1977).

Two remaining cases are less positive: Portugal and Mali. The former became a world empire under the Spanish Hapsburgs, experienced civil war during the nineteenth century, continuing political instability, long-term dictatorship, eventual coup, and establishment of a socialist republic. Despite its authoritarian history, the country has recently experienced fairly peaceful democratic change (Opello 1991). Mali, once the realm of a number of monarchies, was subject to a wide range of external dominance, particularly the French, but achieved early self-rule in 1946, joined a 1959 federation with Senegal, and gained complete independence in 1960 (Snyder 1965). While relatively low in overall conflict, its recent history has included coups and military-backed governments.

Traditional societies which are relatively low in conflict, then, include those who resisted external domination, becoming largely democratic, those attaining internal unity and constitutional monarchies, and those shifting from traditional monarchies to limited political openness. From this it appears clear that independence, national unity, and the decline of absolute rule in traditional societies is crucial to ensuring relatively low levels of intergroup conflict.

Other contexts have not been so harmonious, having been subject to external invasion, manipulation, control, and interference. Egypt, Laos, and Taiwan, for example, were all invaded by external groups, resulting in high levels of different kinds of violence. The first of these, originally ruled by dynasties and autocracies, was invaded by a variety of groups, including the Greeks, Romans, Arabs, Turks, French, and British, eventually becoming a protectorate of the latter in 1914. A monarchy was later established, after which the country experienced a revolution, wars, and assassinations, as well as the influence of the Soviet Union. It remains a rather troubled society, with high levels of potential ethnic conflict (Harris, Ani et al. 1957). Laos has also been through a very troubled history, including external dominance, particularly French influence, later establishment of a constitutional monarch, independence in 1955, and consequent extreme levels of incursions, wars, genocidal dictators, and battles with neighboring countries. The country has been invaded and dominated frequently by neighboring states, including Thailand and Vietnam (Toye 1968). Likewise, Taiwan has been subject to the control of external dynasties, Chinese and Japanese claims, later cession to Japan, limited liberalization, and an ongoing tenuous status in the eyes of the Chinese mainland. While undergoing recent but limited liberalization, the country has entered into negotiations with the mainland regarding its international status (Sih 1973).

Iran, Iraq, and Poland underwent invasion, the establishment of dictatorships, and very high levels of intergroup conflict. Iran was subject to domination by the Greeks, Islam, and British/Russian control, resulting in protectorate status and an imposed monarchy. Outside oil interests played an increasing part in the country's internal affairs, resulting eventually in a revolution against the monarchy and establishment of a rigid theocracy. Its recent history has been violent, both internally and externally, although there are signs of very limited liberalization in the political sphere (Armajani 1972). Iraq, once part of Mesopotamian and Persian empires, was subject to Arab control, Mongolian invasions, Turkish influence, British occupation, and the restoration of the monarchy. A later revolution brought a dictatorship, continuing wars with neighbors and world powers, and internal ethnic conflict. Its recent history, as is well-known, highlights the military threat its regime poses to its neighbors and the world as a whole. This case has also revealed difficulties involved in imposing international sanctions and maintaining effective weapons inspections (Longrigg 1925). Poland was part of a number of regional empires, the Hungarian monarchy, subject to French influence, Stalinist dominance and manipulation, dictators, eventual Solidarity Movement and implementation of a new constitution. The country particularly demonstrates the long-term destructive effects of centuries of external dominance and interference (Halecki 1955). External invasion, manipulation, and support of dictators inevitably results in high levels of destructive strife.

Dictators emerged in a number of other monarchies also, with unfortunate consequences, as can be seen in the case of Ethiopia, France, and the U.S.S.R. The first of these was originally a powerful monarchy which resisted external influences, particularly the British and later the Italians. While other powers such as the French attempted to gain a foothold in the region, they were opposed by a stable, very nationalistic monarchy which eventually defeated outside attempts to gain control over the area. Eventually, however, the monarchy was overthrown by a military revolution and has experienced high levels of consequent violence and deprivation since that time. While originally highly resistant to external interference, this country has recently been subject to regional rebellions and military dictatorships (Rubenson 1976). France, often the target of external invasion, experienced feudalism, various monarchies, political revolution, the Napoleon dictatorship, eventual decline of the monarchy, and emergence of a republic with a strong president. While the scene of a major historical revolution, the society has experienced fairly high levels of internal conflict and limited levels of democratization (Price 1993). Finally, the U.S.S.R., once a Viking state, was invaded often, saw the rise of the Czar and extensive territorial expansion, experienced a number of wars and defeats, the 1917 revolution, and establishment of a number of bloody dictators with genocidal tendencies. While communism has declined significantly recently, this society has a particularly brutal history and recently appears to be declining seriously in regard to its economy, political unity, and daily organization (Hingley 1972).

Other monarchies have been subject to external influence, but resulting in temporary unity, eventually experiencing civil war. These include China, Germany, Japan, and Somalia. China, long embroiled in wars among its feudal states, achieved unification a number of times, undergoing civil wars, north-south fragmentation, Mongol conquest, development of the Manchu Empire, communist revolution, Japanese invasion, and continuing volatility of communist rule. Its continuing authoritarian state tendencies tend to act in opposition to its economic and limited cultural liberalization, resulting in internal and international tension (Cotterell & Morgan 1975). Germany, long ruled by Charlemagne and the Hapsburgs, underwent a variety of civil and external wars, the Reformation, Nazi tragedy, Cold War effects, recent re-unification, and emerging extremist movements. The nation's history reveals a number of conflicts, politically and socially making for volatile times at present (Barraclough 1957). Japan, long ruled by a variety of monarchies and aristocracies, was eventually unified and survived modernization, World War II, American control, economic development, and democratization. Its recent economic turmoil has revealed a number of its institutional and political limitations with respect to effective government (Kennedy 1963). Finally, Somalia, originally a group of independent sultanates, was subject to British control in the north, Italian dominance in the south, a 1949 U.N. Pact involving differential trust areas, ensuing independence and unity in 1960, and regional clan warfare since then, culminating in later U.S. intervention (Lewis 1988). Clearly, imposed unity based on external manipulation results in inevitable and long-term destructive violence. As a poorly integrated multi-ethnic state, this society is highly conflict-ridden in a situation lacking in effective political stability.

Some traditional societies experienced severe external interference in the form of partitioning or mergers. The negative consequences of these arrangements remain evident today. These include situations such as those in Ireland, Israel, Korea, and Syria. The first of these was originally ruled by celtic chiefs, then an Irish monarchy, subject to eventual British control, the 1641 rebellion, 1800 Act of Union, 1920 Home Rule establishing Ulster as North Ireland, 1922 Irish Free State, 1949 republic, and Northern Ireland conflict flaring up in the 1960's, continuing through the present. While a recently-negotiated peace has been implemented in the North, only time will indicate whether it is likely to last in this 'neo-colonial' setting. Since this arrangement institutionalizes rather than removes the partitioning imposed by the colonial past, intergroup violence is likely to continue (White 1968). Israel, as is well-known, was established by a 1947 U.N. partition out of a region originally ruled by monarchies and a wide range of outsiders including the Romans, Palestinians, Mongols, British and eventually Zionists. Arab-Israeli violence has continued ceaselessly since the country's foundation, despite recent attempts at peace and limited Palestinian rule. Since such adjustments do not restore this minority's historical rights, violence is likely to continue (Lewin-Epstein & Seyonov 1993). Korea represents the historical unification of three states dominated by China, creating a number of warring dynasties subject to Chinese and Japanese invasion. Eventual liberation from the latter brought U.S.A. and U.S.S.R. control and trusteeships, international conflict, and the creation of North and South Korea (Hoare & Pares 1988). Regional conflict between the two regions has continued since their original division, recently aggravated by famine, nuclear threats, and missile tests. Finally, Syria, once part of many empires (Persian, Babylonian, Greek, Roman, Islamic, Ottoman, and French) became independent in the 1940s with high levels of political instability. The country merged with Egypt in 1958 only to secede three years later. Since that time, the country has experienced military coups, wars with Israel, and Lebanese intervention. Ruled by a military elite, the country continues to pose a threat to the region as it continues to use its influence to impose on its neighbors (Hitti 1959). Clearly, external manipulation of traditional societies resulting in their partitioning and/or eventual secession creates long-term intergroup hostility and violence.

We turn finally to Turkey, a country which reflects a history of continuous discord. Originally part of a number of empires (Hittite, Greek, Roman, and Ottoman), the society underwent a 1908 rebellion ending sultan control, and resulting in the establishment of a republic in 1923. Since that time, it has experienced high levels of ethnic conflict, World War II, the 1974 Cyprus crisis, a number of civil and military governments, imposition of martial law, and Kurdish conflict with Iraq. The country remains fairly unstable politically, involving a parliamentary system with a powerful president (Price 1956). Based on these case studies, it appears reasonable to conclude that traditional monarchies may proceed through a number of negative intergroup sequences which result in ongoing internal and external violence.

These traditional societies are outlined in Table 9.2 by type of founding contact and level of intergroup conflict. From these results, it is evident that traditional societies (i.e., monarchies, dynasties) may develop historically in a manner which leads either to low or extensive levels of intergroup violence. The former situations include societies who resist external domination and become largely democratic, those who attain internal unity and constitutional monarchies, and those who move away from traditional monarchies towards limited political openness. Violent contexts, on the other hand, have been more subject to external invasion, manipulation, control, and interference. Some societies have been particularly affected by invasions, resulting in high levels of general violence. Others have experienced the establishment of dictatorships in a variety of ways, with unfortunate consequences. Internal unification may result in civil war rather than peace, particularly when imposed and manipulated by outsiders, resulting occasionally in civil war. External partitioning of a country causes inevitable havoc, it would appear, while some contexts with multiple empire backgrounds may experience continuous internal conflict, reflecting the divisive manner in which they were created and manipulated over time. From this it is evident that traditional societies may experience *two* different *types of contact sequences: resistance, unity, and democratization*, producing *lower levels of intergroup conflict* versus *invasion, control, manipulation, and interference behind significantly high levels of intergroup violence and destruction.* The former reflect higher levels of resistance, independence, and democracy while the latter have been negatively affected by external manipulation, control, and interference, reducing their internal freedom, boundaries, and potential levels of equality.

Table 9.2 Traditional Societies by Country, Type of Contact, and Conflict
Level

Countries	Type of Contact	Level of Conflict
Norway, San Marino, Belgium, Netherlands, Austria, Finland	Part of empires which resisted dominance, becoming independent democracies	Low conflict
Sweden, Denmark, Tonga	Developed internal unity and imple-mented constitutional monarchies	Low conflict
Portugal, Mali	Moved from traditional monarchies to indepen-dent self-rule	Low conflict
Egypt, Laos, Taiwan	External invasion, manipulation, control, and interference	High conflict
Iran, Iraq, Poland	External invasion, establishment of dictatorships	High conflict
Ethiopia, France, USSR	Monarchies which resulted in revolutions and establishment of dictatorships	High conflict
China, Germany, Japan, Somalia	Monarchies leading to internal unity and civil war	High conflict
Ireland, Israel, Korea, Syria	External partitioning or mergers	High conflict
Turkey	Part of empires, became a republic with high ethnic conflict, civil and military governments	High conflict

Conclusions

In this chapter we have analyzed intergroup relations in isolated, remote and traditional societies. We found that in the case of the former, isolated or remote areas settled by external refugees, plantation developers, or unusual elites and/or subject to external trust and/or significant economic decline, tended to experience significant levels of political development and democratization, with relatively low levels of intergroup violence. Traditional societies, on the other hand, may encounter two differing types of contact sequences: resistance, unity, and democratization, with lower corollary levels of societal conflict; and, secondly, invasion, control, manipulation, and interference resulting in significantly high levels of violence and destruction. What appears crucial in these analyses is the degree to which a particular society's independence and political development are facilitated or impeded by outside forces.

We turn to examine nations subject to direct external control and invasion.

10

Intergroup Relations Worldwide: Societies Subject to External Control and Invasion

In this chapter we shall examine intergroup relations in countries subject to direct external control and invasion, with either peaceful or violent consequences, depending on the major kinds of contact involved, particularly in each society's foundation.

Societies Subject to Direct External Control

Not all countries subject to direct external control reveal high levels of violence; many have had their security guaranteed by other powers in a number of ways. These include Andorra, Liechtenstein, Luxembourg, Monaco, and Switzerland. The first of these was originally a small, isolated feudal state, eventually a co-principality of Spain and France, which was influenced by external rivalries, invasions, and an influx of refugees, but has maintained its independence and remains relatively unique for its lack of poverty, absence of bureaucracy, high levels of equalitarianism, and relative lack of conflict, most of which remains external. It is clearly a unique society in many remarkable respects (Playfair & FitzGibbon 1954). Liechtenstein emerged out of the Holy Roman Empire in 1806 to become a principality with an absolute monarchy tied to the Austro-Hungarian monarchy, maintaining its independence and neutrality, for the most part, eventually becoming a liberal democracy. This nation is also unique for the manner in which even the Nazis respected its independence (Kranz 1967). It has experienced significant levels of industrialization, acts as a major corporate site, and has kept out of major international conflicts. Similarly, Luxembourg was originally part of the Holy Roman Empire, was influenced by Spain, eventually coming under control of the Netherlands in 1815. In 1867 its independence was guaranteed by a London Conference. Later occupied by Germany, it has remained a peaceful duchy with a high level of democracy, political stability, and economic development. Its history of guaranteed sovereignty, political stability, and high level of democracy is relatively unique also (Newcomer 1984). Monaco was also originally dominated by a variety of outsiders, including the Greeks, Phoenicians, Romans, French, Spanish, and Italians; however, their influence was largely protective while their own form of government eventually shifted from absolute to constitutional monarchy (Hudson 1991). Long famous for its casinos, the country remains a major peaceful tourist attraction in the region. Finally, Switzerland, renown for its long history of local autonomy, neutrality, and independence, was once a Roman province subject to outside invasions but had its independence guaranteed by the 1815 Treaty of Vienna. In 1315 a federation of cantons was established to preserve its tradition of freedom and its impressively high levels of local autonomy, militancy, tourism, and democracy (reflected in a rotating presidency) have been maintained ever since (Schmid 1981). Switzerland remains one of the world's most impressive examples of local independence, societal unity, neutrality, and intergroup harmony, despite its militant past. These particular cases demonstrate that relatively small, homogeneous, isolated societies whose independence and neutrality are protected and guaranteed by outsiders tend to experience relatively low levels of intergroup conflict. External domination and control under particular circumstances may facilitate rather than reduce indigenous independence and harmony.

Mongolia and Vanuatu also illustrate how external support may facilitate internal independence. The former was originally a feudal state under Genghis Khan in the thirteenth century, an empire which eventually dissolved, eventually bringing the country under Chinese rule. During the 1911 Chinese Revolution, part of Mongolia declared its independence from China but was unsuccessful. Later U.S.S.R. support brought Chinese recognition of their new status in the 1940s but subject to the former's powerful control of the country. The Communist Party eventually declined in 1990 and the region has moved towards democracy and a more open economy (Bawden 1968). While not lacking periods of significant conflict, the society has been aided by outsiders in its struggle against Chinese domination with positive results eventually. Its relative cultural and religious homogeneity is remarkable also. Vanuatu, a very different kind of society, was originally explored by the Spanish, French, and British, subject to sandalwood and labor exploitation, as well as missionary influence, eventually coming under the control of a joint British/French naval commission. Later events included avoidance of Japanese occupation, temporary New Zealand control, and eventual independence, with very limited levels of violence (Douglas & Douglas 1986). Despite external control and exploitation, the society has remained remarkably low in violence. Again, these situations illustrate how outsiders may facilitate eventual indigenous independence and relatively low levels of conflict under certain circumstances, despite related negative conditions.

Other situations subject to external control have been far less harmonious, involving the emergence of dictators, manipulative monarchies, and/or relatively high levels of intergroup conflict. The Philippines, Malawi, Cambodia, and Papua New Guinea are major examples. The first of these, originally a group of Malayan principalities, fell to sixteenth century Spanish conquest, experienced an 1896 uprising, and was ceded to the United States in 1898, after which it was subject to their continuous control, achieving U.S. commonwealth and then independent status in the 1930's and 1940's. The region suffered at the hands of the Japanese in World War II and then a twenty-year dictatorship beginning in the 1960s, after which democratization, combined with coups and corruption, occurred. U.S. base withdrawals have complicated the country's economic problems while these islands continue to reveal high levels of intergroup conflict and economic instability. Generally, this society has a history of external conquest, exploitation, and very limited economic development, resulting in severe long-term social problems, reflecting its 'neo-colonial' status (Shalom 1981). Malawi, once under Portuguese and then British dominance, eventually became a protectorate of the latter in 1891, subject to missionary influence and plantation development. Temporarily part of a regional federation in the 1960s, nationalist movements facilitated the country's early withdrawal from this arrangement and independence under a long-term indigenous and very repressive dictator. Its history of external exploitation and internal dictatorship is reflected in its negative intergroup relations (Pachai 1973). Cambodia has been an even more bloody society: originally three independent tribes, this region was subject to Malayan influence, Mongol control, French dominance, Japanese influence, eventual independence from the French with a republican government then monarchy whose abdication reflected the country's continuing political and social instability. Its civil wars and genocidal "reigns of terror" continued to illustrate its long tradition of severe intergroup violence. Again, a history of multiple external control, exploitation, political instability, and civil wars reveals its very negative continuity (Steinberg, Bain, et al. 1959). Finally, Papua New Guinea, a very different historical context, nevertheless was subject to a number of outside powers including the Dutch, German, British, Japanese, and Australian. These islands were occupied by the latter in 1914, later invaded by the Japanese, and subject to a U.N. Australian mandate, achieving independence in 1975 with continuing Australian influence and intergroup conflict reflected in ongoing guerilla clashes. Multiple outside forces have done little to ensure its internal harmony and stability (Griffin, Nelson & Firth 1979). In these cases, then, external control, manipulation, and exploitation have often resulted in negative political arrangements and significant levels of intergroup conflict, often to highly destructive degrees.

The above societies are summarized in Table 10.1 by type of contact and conflict level. They tend to illustrate that societies subject to direct external control may experience relatively *low levels of intergroup violence* when their *security is guaranteed* by outside powers *or their independence is facilitated by them.* However, *outside manipulation and exploitation* may *aggravate potential violence* through their contribution to the *establishment of negative political arrangements, particularly dictatorships, unstable monarchies, or trusts.* Again, similar contributing factors or types of intergroup contact may operate in different ways: outside powers may facilitate *either* independence and harmony *or* exploitation

Table 10.1   Societies Subject to Direct External Control by Country, Type of
             Contact, and Conflict Level

Countries	Type of Contact	Level of Conflict
Andorra, Luxembourg, Monaco, Switzerland	Independence and neutrality guaranteed by external powers	Low conflict
Mongolia, Vanuatu	External support for internal independence	Low conflict
Philippines, Malawi, Cambodia, Papua New Guinea	External control, manipulation, and exploitation producing negative political arrangements	High conflict

and violence. The particular intergroup contacts and sequences
involved in these situations are crucial to what eventuates. We
turn to examine situations subject to external invasion.

Societies Subject To External Invasion

While invasions may appear inevitably to produce high levels of
intergroup conflict, this is not *always* the situation. A case in point
is Tuvalu, a group of Polynesian Pacific islands subject to the influence of whalers, traders, labor recruiters, and missionaries,
eventually becoming a British colony in 1915. Significantly, this
small society was not occupied by the Japanese during World War
II, achieving self-rule in 1971 and independence in 1978. U.S.
claims to some of the islands were also dropped a year later in ex-
change for military access to the area. The country has developed
demographically and economically in relative peace with high levels of local independence (Oliver 1951). While subject to outside invasions, this isolated area has developed fairly peacefully over
time.

Other situations have not been as fortunate, instead experiencing
external control, imposed monarchies and dictatorships, emergence of revolutions, partitioning, and civil war. Often, outside invasions result in significant levels of intergroup violence. This was
particularly so in the case of Bulgaria, Italy, Morocco, and Thailand.
The first of these was subject to a number of invasions, including

the Turks and later U.S.S.R., Greek control, communist domination, eventual socialism, and high levels of civil conflict. Lacking in freedom and independence, it is little wonder its history has been so conflict-ridden (Anastasoff 1977). Italy experienced Roman and German invasions as well as Napoleonic control, becoming a kingdom in 1861 with high rates of ongoing strife. Twentieth century developments included fascist rule, Hitler's influence, and high levels of post-war economic problems and political conflict. stability of any kind has remained largely absent in this highly popular tourist mecca (Gunn 1971). Morocco was invaded by the Berbers, Phoenicians, Romans, Vandals, Islamic groups, Mauritanian dominance, and both Spanish and French influence. Unity under a monarchy was established in the eighth century, eventually becoming a constitutional monarchy in more recent times. The country has continued to experience very high levels of ethnic and other types of intergroup conflict, despite implementation of a new constitution (Barbour 1966). Finally, Thailand, originally a number of states, was subject to Indian influence, restored its monarchy in the eighteenth century, was occupied by the Japanese during World War II, and has experienced limited democratic and military rule since, with very high levels of intergroup violence. Recent military interference in the political process and their repressive treatment of dissidents have aggravated intergroup tension considerably (Suwannathat-Pian 1988). These societies clearly demonstrate that high numbers of outside invasions, subsequent control and manipulation and establishment of dictators and monarchies tend to result in conflict-ridden contexts whose negative intergroup relations continue through today.

A number of countries have experienced even higher numbers of invasions, external domination, wars, establishment of monarchies and dictators, and continuously high levels of intergroup violence. These include Afghanistan, Albania, Greece, Hungary, Libya, Romania, Spain, and Tunisia. The first of these, a major cross-road in that part of the world, suffered at the hands of at least eight invaders, including the Greeks, Indians, Iranians, Persians, Turks, Mongols, British, and Soviets. The Afghan throne was established, further aggravating potential conflict, while ethnic political dominance eventually resulted in a military coup and Russian involvement in the country's civil war. Recently taken over by sectarian rebels, the country has appeared to go from bad to worse, with a war with neighboring Iran a distinct possibility (Wilber, Bacon et al. 1962). Albania was subject to Greek, Turkish, and Italian dominance, with its history including a self-proclaimed monarch, socialist dictatorship, continuing outside interference, ongoing conflict, and a recent revolution (Marmullaku 1975). Recently, potential conflict with neighboring states has increased also, aggravating an already destructive situation. Greece, despite its democratic tradition, reflects very high levels of outside domination, wars, combined with internal monarchies, dictators, juntas, and extremely high levels of intergroup conflict (Woodhouse 1968). Ironically, this birthplace of democracy has one of the most repressive histories in Europe. Hungary, originally consisting of seven unified tribes, has been subject to Turkish, Hapsburg, Austrian, Russian, and Stalinist invasions and domination. While democracy has recently emerged, the society's history is extremely bloody and unstable, reflecting a number of extremely brutal regimes imposed externally (Volgyes 1981). Libya, invaded by the Byzantines, Ottomans, Italians, and French eventually became a protectorate with a constitutional monarch. A 1969 military coup turned the society into a revolutionary dictatorship, with extremely high levels of violence, both internally and internationally, ever since. Its continuing terrorist support has only worsened its position in the worldwide community (Wright 1982). Romania was also controlled by a wide range of outsiders, including the Romans, Bulgars, Mongols, Ottomans, Greeks, and Russians, suffering through conflict-ridden monarchies, dictators, economic decline, and satellite status. A recent revolution has improved conditions somewhat but the society remains largely problematic (Bobango 1979). Spain was also subject to the influence of at least ten outside countries, combined with internal dictators, civil war, attempted coups, and eventually a socialist state (Vilar 1967). Part of a number of dominions during its history, the country eventually created an extensive state bureaucracy and colonial empire. Throughout all of this, its level of intergroup conflict, internally and externally, politically and religiously-speaking, has remained significantly high. Finally, Tunisia experienced a wide range of external domination also, including the Phoenicians, Romans, Vandals, Byzantines, Islamic invaders, Turks, and French, achieving independence in 1956, only to be invaded by the Libyans not long after. With its socialist government and nationalized economy, the country continues to be the scene of ongoing political unrest and strife (Micaud 1964). These societies clearly illustrate the degree to which external invasions, domination, and imposed rulers are highly correlated with continuous intergroup violence.

Occasionally external invasions, control, and claims may result in indigenous revolts and crises. Jordan and Namibia exemplify such situations. The former experienced the rule of the Greeks, Romans, Arabs, Crusaders, Turks, and eventually British who controlled the area by mandate. Later developments included an established monarchy, independence in 1946, constitutional rule, rebellions, East/West Bank unification, and continuing political crises (Harris, Ani et al. 1958). The country's relations with its varied neighbors remain complicated and somewhat unstable. Namibia, on the other hand, was occupied by the British, subject to destructive German claims, South African rule under U.N. mandate, the former's resistance to withdrawal, and an indigenous nationalist movement which, after a war, achieved full independence in 1990 (Fraenkel & Murray, 1985).

Other societies, such as Mexico and the United Kingdom, with monarchies and subsequent revolutions, differ in the emergence of a dominant middle class which eventually controls the political system. The former, as is well-known, was dominated by Spanish colonists, emperors, dictators, and very high levels of conflict, including internal uprisings, wars with the United States, external intervention, a revolution, land and constitutional reform, and emergence of middle class political dominance and economic development (Rodman 1982). Recent financial problems, drug wars, and indigenous terrorism reflect the continuing degree to which this context is highly problematic and conflict-ridden. The United Kingdom, once a group of Celtic states, was invaded by the Romans, Vikings, and Saxons, and subject to monarchical rule. The 1215 Magna Carta increased the power of the nobility in the face of this royal power, resulting eventually in a constitutional monarchy, parliamentary democracy, industrial expansion, rise of union power, and development of the welfare state (Bryant 1954). While a democracy emphasizing religious, political, and legal rights, this country has experienced very high levels of intergroup conflict throughout its long history, some of which continues in Northern Ireland. While devolution may help diffuse some of these tensions, Anglo-Saxon dominance will guarantee their continuing expression in varying forms. Ironically, while most of the British Empire has experienced de-colonization, much of the United Kingdom has not.

Finally, external invasions and control may produce partitioning and eventual civil war: Lebanon and Vietnam are two major examples. The former was the scene of Persian, Roman, Byzantine, Islamic, Syrian, Ottoman, British, and French control, aggravating Maronite and Druze conflict, subject to 1918 partitioning under French mandate. Civil and external wars have been constant in this situation, essentially an artificially created state carved out of the Ottoman Empire by the British and French (Salibi 1988). While relative political stability has returned recently, the country has far to go in establishing a peaceful-based society. Vietnam is an even more extreme example: originally a Hindu-Buddhist kingdom, the region has been subject to Chinese expansion, French dominance, Japanese occupation, outside manipulation of the monarchy, partitioning, a war with the United States, reunification, and recent conflict with Cambodia and China (Hanh 1967). While recently undergoing economic development in the international context, this country is extremely far from being a peaceful democracy. These particular cases demonstrate vividly what when partitioning is effected in the context of external invasion and control, civil war appears inevitable.

The above societies are summarized in Table 10.2 by contact type and level of conflict. Subject to external invasion, they tend to fare poorly with respect to consequent intergroup relations. While isolated *situations not subject to occupation whose independence is facilitated* and *subject to negotiation* may *not experience high levels of intergroup violence, societies* formed *through external incursion, control, imposition of monarchies and dictators, and subject to partitioning in some cases, invariably experience severe levels of intergroup conflict, including revolutions and civil war.* Obviously, outside dominance and manipulation are extremely damaging to a society's internal relations. While this may not be the case in *every* situation, it applies to the overwhelming majority of them.

Conclusions

This chapter has found that nations subject to direct external control may experience relatively low levels of intergroup conflict when their security is guaranteed by outside powers or their independence is facilitated by them. Outside manipulation and exploitation, on the other hand, may aggravate potential violence through their encouragement of negative political arrangements such as dictatorships, unstable monarchies, or trusts. We also discovered that societies not subject to occupation whose independence is facilitated and subject to negotiation may be relatively harmonious in contrast to those formed through external incursion, control, imposed monarchies or dictators, or subject to partitioning, who invariably undergo severe violence, including revolutions and civil war. According to these results, external facilitation of independence produces intergroup harmony while severe interference, manipulation, and imposed arrangements tend to result in bloodshed and destructive violence.

We turn to examine societies subject to the highest levels of outside dominance: protectorates and colonies.

Table 10.2   Societies Subject to External Invasion by Country, Type of Contact, and Conflict Level

Countries	Type of Contact	Level of Conflict
Tuvalu	Not occupied and external claims dropped	Low conflict
Bulgaria, Italy, Morocco, Thailand	External control, imposed monarchies and dictatorships, with emerging revolutions, partitioning, and civil war	High conflict
Afghanistan, Albania, Greece, Hungary, Libya, Romania, Spain, Tunisia	External invasions, domination, wars, with establishment of monarchies and dictators	High conflict
Jordan, Namibia	External invasions, control, and claims leading to indigenous crises and revolts	High conflict
Mexico, United Kingdom	Monarchies, revolutions, and emergence of dominant middle classes	High conflict
Lebanon, Vietnam	External invasions and control resulting in partitioning and civil war	High conflict

11

Intergroup Relations Worldwide: Protectorates and Colonies

In this chapter we turn to countries subject to protectorate or colonial status (some of the most extreme forms of external control and exploitation), imposed by outsiders, with differential results, once again.

Societies Subject To Protectorate Status

A number of societies ruled by traditional elites became protectorates, particularly of Great Britain, with their autocracies and royal bureaucracies largely intact. While these are far from democratic and may encounter future conflict, their levels of general violence have remained relatively low. These include Bahrain, Bhutan, Brunei, Kiribati, Kuwait, the Maldive Islands, Oman, Qatar, Saudi Arabia, and the United Arab Emirates. The first of these originated as an emirate, subject to Portuguese and Turkish influence. In the nineteenth century the area became a British protectorate, gaining its independence in 1971 ruled by a constitutional monarchy (Lawson 1989). With its oil economy, the country has undergone significant economic development and remains a fairly peaceful autocracy, although the parliament was dissolved in 1987. Bhutan was a Buddhist theocracy, largely inaccessible for many years, with a heredity monarchy, palace bureaucracy, national assembly, high linguistic tolerance, low levels of poverty, and peaceful modernization, experiencing low levels of internal conflict. Given its inaccessible location, internal unity, British protection, and gradual rate of social change, its relatively harmonious situation is not surprising, perhaps (Rose 1977). Brunei, a sultanate, has remained relatively free of outside domination, ruled by an aristocratic, monarchist elite which has maintained its political power. The country experienced British economic influence and eventual protectorate status but has largely maintained its traditional social arrangements despite pressures to change. Significantly, its sultanate has remained relatively free of external interference and domination (Singh 1984). Kiribati, formerly the Gilbert Islands, was a traditional patriarchy administered by the British both as a protectorate and then colony, with relatively high levels of local autonomy. They have experienced peaceful modernization, achieving self-rule in 1971 and later withdrawal from their federal status. As with other countries in this category, they have managed to retain their local autonomy for much of their history, subject to British protection and economic aid (Sabatier 1977). Kuwait, long ruled by an elite family, was influenced by the Turks and British, eventually becoming a protectorate of the latter, under whose influence a royal family and bureaucratic state have flourished. The country represents an extremely rich, traditional state which has experienced gradual, largely conflict-free modernization (Crystal 1990). Independence was achieved in 1961 with a national assembly subject to monarchical power. The Maldive Islands, located off India, were influenced by a wide variety of outsiders, eventually converting to Islam and becoming a British protectorate in 1887. They later gained independence and abolished the sultanate (Maloney 1980). While generally lacking in intergroup violence, they have recently experienced political unrest and attempted coups. Their indigenous culture has remained surprisingly intact in the face of outside influences. Oman, ruled by sultans, was subject to Egyptian, Roman, Persian, Portuguese, Turkish, and then British influence. The country eventually became a British protectorate in the nineteenth century, achieving independence in the following century (Clements 1980). The British helped the sultanate quash any threatening internal rebellions in this traditional state. A strong monarchy continues to rule a society supported primarily by an oil economy. Qatar, ruled by sheiks, was controlled by the Turks and then the British, eventually developing an elaborate bureaucracy under the royal family's control (Crystal 1990). While significant expansion of medical and educational facilities has occurred, emerging working class opposition has resulted in limited protests and controversy, bringing about limited societal reforms. Saudi Arabia, similarly subject to Turkish and British influence, eventually became a British protectorate also, expanding its territory and oil economy using foreign workers, and has recently experienced internal religious conflict and rising U.S. pressures. Its history reflects the rise of Saudi power with British help, creating a largely patrimonial regime as a result (Kostiner 1993). Finally, the United Arab Emirates, a group of seven sheikdoms, likewise became a British protectorate, eventually formed an independent federation, and has flourished with its powerful oil industry and sheikdoms at its center (Khalifa 1979). Generally, the society has experienced little internal conflict despite outside pressures for social change. The country's vital role in the global oil economy has, perhaps, been a major factor in this trend. In general, these traditional societies, protected by the British, have largely retained their royal elites, bureaucracies, and autocratic political arrangements, undergoing economic development and modernization with little outward sign of internal conflict. While some of these regimes remain absolutist, others involve a combination of traditional monarchies and advisory councils which provide their rulers with limited advice. Absence of apparent conflict, however, should *not* be taken as a sign of permanent peace: social and economic pressures may result in significant violence at a later date. For the present, however, these regions, protected and aided by outside powers, particularly the British, have remained largely homogeneous, prosperous, and peaceful.

Some of these cases have developed further politically, achieving impressive levels of democratization. This occurred in Botswana, Lesotho, Swaziland, and Burkina Faso, all of which were subject to British dominance also. The first of these, a self-sufficient indigenous kingdom, fought with the South African Boers, became a British protectorate, thereafter instituting tribal government, advisory councils, interracial councils, and a legislative council before becoming a parliamentary democracy in 1966. The country is a major example of the positive effects of external influences on a traditional society which resists external domination and gradually undergoes democratization (Sillery 1974). Lesotho was formed out of a tribal amalgamation as a powerful kingdom who appealed to the British for protection against invading whites, were annexed to the latter in 1868, and experienced the indirect rule of the Cape Government, eventually gaining independence in 1966 (Bardill & Cobbe 1985). While the country has experienced increasingly authoritarian types of control, its general level of intergroup conflict has remained relatively low, although recent factionalism has resulted in rebellion, rioting, and outside intervention by neighboring South Africa. Nevertheless, while reflect internal divisions, the country's overall level of conflict remains quite limited. Swaziland became a unified kingdom in the nineteenth century, was later controlled by the British, eventually establishing a constitutional monarchy but subject to the incursions of South African whites attacking nationalist groups in the area. Since independence, the country has maintained a parliamentary democracy (Bonner 1982). In these cases, countries ruled by traditional elites and protected by the British from the attacks of neighbors, have moved peacefully towards implementing democratic political arrangements within these more autocratic-type contexts. Burkina Faso (formerly the Upper Volta) is another positive example: a traditional empire which became a French protectorate, the country experienced both educational and limited political development, achieving self-government and then independence in 1960. Political unrest, including military rules, coups, and limited conflict followed; however, limited political reconciliation was achieved, only to be later followed by dictatorial and one-party rule (McFarland 1978). While this country represents a limited case, its achievement of relatively non-violence post-coup reconciliation remains significant, as are its limited political reforms implemented since one-party rule was established. Accordingly, under some circumstances, protectorates may flourish economically and politically, either in the form of modified autocracies or limited democracies.

Not all such situations are positive, however: protectorates may involve slavery, regional divisions, and plantation exploitation, resulting in long-term conflict. Madagascar, Togo, and Benin are major examples of the latter situation. The first of these was originally founded by Indonesian and migrants from Malaysia, proceeding through an indigenous, centralized monarchy, failed Portuguese colonialism, temporary British influence, and eventually establishment of a French protectorate. The latter were extremely harsh in their exploitation of forced labor, resulting eventually in a rebellion, later independence, a Marxist coup, repressive regimes, high levels of ethnic conflict, and, recently, more moderate political situations. In general, the society reflects and continues to reveal its violent past (Covell 1987).Togo was controlled by the Portuguese during the fourteenth century, being part of the slave coast during later centuries, becoming a German protectorate in 1884, subject to post–World War I mandates in which the country was split between the British (in the west) and French (controlling the eastern part), resulting eventually in independence, a military coup, and recent democratic movements. Its history tends to be generally exploitive and problematic (Curkeet 1993). Benin, once the realm of warring princes, was influenced by Portuguese traders, the slave trade, became a French protectorate, eventually entered a federation, and achieved republican status in 1960 with very high levels of political instability, including a revolutionary government. Again, a history of regionalism, exploitation, and external control tends to reinforce high and continuing levels of intergroup conflict (Manning 1982). Clearly, protectorates subject to forced labor and slavery tend to have conflict-ridden histories.

Some protectorates were divided into different regions by race: Mauritania was one of these. Once part of a number of kingdoms, the north was dominated by Arabs, the south predominantly African. The French, British, and Dutch all competed for influence in the area which became a French protectorate and colony, eventually achieving self-government and independence. Since then, the country has experienced conflict with Morocco, a military coup, and continuing racial and ethnic conflict. Its background of diversity, invasions, and external control are reflected in its ongoing problems (Gerteiny 1967). Outside manipulation of a region by ethnicity and geography appears to produce inevitable conflict.

Finally, traditional monarchies supported by outsiders may also result in high levels of internal violence. Nepal is a limited case in point: eventually unified as Gurhka kingdom, the country signed a treaty with the British in 1792. Royal intrigue, massacres, violence, armed revolution, and riots followed, with limited political reforms, resulting in the establishment of a constitutional monarchy and prime minister with executive power (Joshi & Rose 1966). While conflict has not approached extremely high levels since that time, the country's history is far from harmonious, including riots and the maintenance of executive political controls.

Viewing the above societies as a whole, it appears that protectorates imposed by outside powers may have either positive or negative consequences for those within them. In the former case, such status enables traditional elites to maintain themselves as autocracies and bureaucratic states in the face of modernization, with limited levels of conflict. Some may even become democracies or constitutional monarchies while still others appear able to reconcile their differences despite periods of turbulence. However, outside exploitation of protectorates using forced labor and other forms of slavery have much more negative consequences. External manipulation of regions by race or significant support of negative monarchies may also aggravate potential intergroup violence.

The above societies are outlined in Table 11.1 by formative contact type and conflict level. In general, it appears that traditional societies may be facilitated as *adaptive autocracies* and *bureaucratic states* by outside powers, resulting in *political and economic stability* in the face of inevitable change. However, when protectorate status involves *economic exploitation through forced labor and slavery, regional manipulation*, and *support for negative traditional elites, negative intergroup relations tend to follow, including high levels of intergroup violence*. We should also emphasize that even some of the more positive situations outlined above might result eventually in severe conflict if they fail to adapt successfully to inevitable pressures for economic, political, and social change. We turn, finally, to societies subject to the most negative type of external exploitation—colonial situations.

Colonial Societies

Given that colonized societies have frequently been subject to the most destructive external treatment, they are often the most violent of all. This, however, is not always the case: some have included indigenous political development, development of self-rule, significant levels of economic growth, and generally low degrees of intergroup conflict. Nevertheless, their colonial status should be kept in mind, whatever their surface appearance: *potential* or *imbedded inequities*, based on their historical formation,

Table 11.1 Societies Subject to Protectorate Status by Country, Type of Contact, and Conflict Level

Countries	Type of Contact	Level of Conflict
Bahrain, Bhutan, Brunei, Kiribati, Kuwait, Maldive Islands, Oman, Qatar, Saudi Arabia, United Arab Emirates	Traditional elites whose autocracies and bureaucracies remain intact under protectorate status	Low conflict
Botswana, Lesotho, Swaziland, Burkina Faso	Democratic political development under protectorate status	Low conflict
Madagascar, Togo, Benin	Slavery, regional divisions, plantation exploitation under protectorate status	High conflict
Mauritania	Protectorate divided into regions by race	High conflict
Nepal	Traditions monarchy supported by outsiders	High conflict

might rise to the forefront under future competitive circumstances, creating significant intergroup strife at that time. Relatively-speaking, and for the moment, however, they appear generally peaceful. Examples include Gambia, Guinea, the Ivory Coast, Malta, New Zealand, Senegal, and Tanzania. The first of these was subject to Portuguese, French, and British influence, the slave trade, Muslim and civil wars, eventually ruled indirectly by the British, achieving self-rule in 1963 (Gailey 1975). Constitutionally, the country began independence including traditional chiefs in its constitution, removing them later, and generally instituting civil rights in a manner which maintained societal harmony. This is clearly remarkable in a nation involving significant levels of ethnic pluralism. Guinea, also affected by the slave trade, Muslims, indirect rule, in this case by the French, was granted independence in 1958 with a history of indigenous political participation (O'Toole 1978). Its recent history has included socialism, purges, political conflict, and economic change; however, it has remained largely free from destructive conflict. Again, this is unusual in lights of the country's diverse population. The Ivory Coast's history includes French missionaries and trading posts, high levels of indigenous resistance, plantation development, French colonialism and exploitation with forced labor, and continuing indigenous political activity, culminating in the country's 1960 independence (Mundt 1987). Since that time, the region has experienced limited political conflict combined with high levels of economic growth. Its recent history of union leadership and encouragement is particularly interesting. Malta, a Mediterranean cross-road, has been the scene of very high levels of outside invasion, with increasing French influence and then British annexation in 1841. The islands were granted limited self-rule, with full independence from the British in 1971. Subsequently, the region has experienced significant economic growth and limited church-state conflict, but not to any destructive extent. While subject to multiple invasions, this interesting case reveals gradual local independence and a general lack of intergroup violence (Dobie 1967). New Zealand, originally settled by migrating Maoris, was claimed by Cook in the eighteenth century, eventually becoming a British colony in 1841 with the former's final defeat. Dominion status was granted in 1907 with full independence within the commonwealth later. While its history includes earlier wars with the indigenous population and ongoing conflict over Maori land rights, it has generally remained largely peaceful (Sinclair 1980). Senegal, once part of ancient empires, was subject to European competition for dominance, eventually becoming a French possession. The country achieved self-rule in 1958, with full independence in 1960. Its recent history has included attempted coups, riots, federation with and secession from local countries, and emerging socialism. Despite its history of significant external influences and exploitation, the country has not revealed high levels of violent conflict (Colvin 1981). Finally, Tanzania, representing the combination of formerly Tanganyika and Zanzibar, has a history of German, Portuguese, and British involvement, Sultan control in the case of the latter, British mandates, limited colonial domination, 1964 unity as Tanzania, an emerging socialist state, and recent multiparty secularism (Kurtz 1978). Its recent history, while involving significant economic problems, has remained largely peaceful under impressive political leadership, all of which is highly impressive in lights of its colonial, exploitive past. In general, these cases are insightful in indicating that, despite subject to colonial domination and severe exploitation in some cases, societies who include high levels of indigenous resistance to external influence, positive economic growth (in some instances), and maintain majority political development are not generally subject to high levels of intergroup violence.

Some demonstrate outstanding economic development, such as Djibouti and Gabon. The former, essentially the "horn of Africa," was explored by European traders and scientists, coming under increasing French influence with colonial status imposed peacefully in 1888 in the face of tribal hostility. While affected by the two world wars and Italian conflict in the area, the society underwent significant economic development, becoming independent in 1977. Multiparty elections occurred in 1992 and the country has remained generally peaceful since that time. Impressive, once again, is the relative lack of destructive violence is a highly colonial, diverse society subject to significant levels of external influence (Thompson & Adloff 1968). Gabon, earlier explored by Portuguese traders, came under increasing nineteenth century French dominance, including a slave trade, imported plantation labor, high levels of abuse, and economic decline, with eventual independence in 1960, continuing French intervention, an autocratic regime, and labor unrest (Gardinier 1994). However, significant economic development has occurred since, particularly for the country's elite, with limited political reforms implemented, including multiparty elections. Overall, the society has not been the scene of high levels of violence on a conti; uous basis. Despite imported plantation labor, various colonial abuses, outside military intervention and support for elite regimes, the country has remained relatively peaceful.

Australia and Canada are major examples of colonies controlled by middle class elites which eventually become thriving democracies. The former was explored by the Dutch then subject to British claims and used as a penal colony. Separate sub-states developed within the continent, during which the indigenous population was largely destroyed. Later developments included an 1851 gold rush, high rates of immigration, 1901 commonwealth government, and immigration policy liberalization in the 1970s. While the society represents a welfare state, its aboriginal population remains largely poverty-stricken. Generally, however, this 'radical' or 'proletarian' colony (Hartz 1964), has been largely lacking in violent intergroup conflict (Stanner 1971). Canada, originally explored by traders, was founded on British/French rivalry with the eventual defeat of the latter who retained their cultural traditions and institutions. The country became a federation with high levels of local independence, eventually becoming a constitutional monarchy with a strong democratic tradition (Brebner 1960). While its history is largely peaceful, ethnic tension with Quebec continues, while native rights and related conflict continue to fester in the society generally. Nevertheless, such developments do not detract significantly from its relatively peaceful past.

We turn finally in this group to Dominica, a Caribbean island with an interesting background. Affected by hostile Caribs and Spanish slave raids, the area was eventually settled by the French, then captured by the British, resulting in increasing slavery and conflict with the Caribs. High levels of white/black racial mixing occurred, however, and the region has experienced very low levels of political nationalism. Achieving independence in 1978, the country remains peaceful but high in poverty and low in economic development. While its history has been relatively negative, its intergroup relations have not been highly violent on a continuous basis (Layng 1983).

Colonialism is *always* destructive in some manner and to a particular degree: its influence on indigenous and migrant groups, resource arrangements, the ecology, and subsequent intergroup relations is problematic to *some* extent. However, such consequences vary by context and do not always include destructive levels of social violence, as these particular countries illustrate. When indigenous resistance and political development, self-rule, significant levels of economic growth, emergence of middle-class elites, and high levels of miscegenation occur in colonial contexts, more democratic, less conflict-ridden intergroup relations tend to follow. While this is not *always* the case, *nor* does it imply that future violence will not occur based on endemic forms of stratification, such variations are significant to fuller understanding of the contextual nature of intergroup strife. We turn to consider the more typical consequences of colonial domination: high levels of societal violence.

We have previously emphasized that colonialism typically consists of external migration, subordination of indigenous populations, expropriation of their resources, and importation of outside groups for labor purposes (Kinloch 1974). The negative consequences of this process are wide-ranging, including the creation of new, manipulated minorities, use of forced labor for economic exploitation of the colony, emergence of often autocratic elites, and other forms of external exploitation. Conflict-ridden intergroup relations ensue inevitably from such developments.

Often colonialism involves the external imposition and manipulation of unequal types of pluralism or minorities, resulting in the emergence of dictatorships, civil war, and continuing intergroup violence. Such a process has been involved in the formation of a large number of societies worldwide, ranging from Myanmar (formerly Burma) to Uganda. The first of these emerged out of earlier dynasties, Chinese invasions, international competition for dominance, British annexation, separation from India, Japanese control, 1948 independence, and high levels of coups, military control, and political violence since that time, explicable in light of the country's significant degrees of ethnic, linguistic, and religious diversity. The country has recent gained notoriety due to the military regime's treatment of dissidents (Aung 1967). Burundi was particularly subject to outside interference, including German attempts to divide and rule the area, Belgian manipulation of the Tutsi versus Hutus, incorporation into a Ruanda-Burundi Trust, accelerated independence in 1962, and continuing ethnic violence, often to genocidal degrees, since that time. In this case, the genocidal consequences of colonial divide and manipulate are particularly evident (Lemarchand 1970). The Belgians and French also competed for dominance of the Central African Republic, resulting eventually in French control, exploitation, and labor abuses. The society's post-independence political events have included multiple coups, military regimes, and economic disaster in a setting consisting of at least eight different ethnic groups. Again, colonial competition and exploitation have extremely damaging consequences for the society as a whole (Kalek 1971). Chad is another example of disastrous French colonialism: once governed by chiefs, the country was subject to Arab raids and nineteenth century French penetration, eventually dividing the region into two areas—the north primarily Islamic Arabs, the south predominantly African. Independence brought a destructive civil war, eventual peace conferences, continuing conflict, and limited political reform. Here, regional division and colonial exploitation have resulted in very negative historical consequences (Thompson & Adloff 1981). The Congo, also an arena of French influence, originally three tribal kingdoms, was affected by slave traders, increasing French domination, exploitation, forced labor, land alienation, and other abuses, becoming independent in 1960, with consequent coups, military governments, and tribal rioting. Again, this represents yet another negative, conflict-ridden type of society (McDonald, Bernier, et al. 1971). Czechoslovakia, formed out of the unequal unification of the Czechs and Slovaks in 1918, put the latter at a disadvantage which, combined with continuing outside interference, resulted in continuing intergroup conflict until the recent establishment of a Czech Republic in 1993 (Leff 1988). While not a typically colonial situation, this country clearly illustrates the destructive effects of imposed, unequal ethnic unification, resulting in continuing strife and inequality.

Other typical colonial situations include Kenya, Nigeria, Rwanda, Sri Lanka, the Sudan, and Uganda. The first of these came under increasing British dominance in the nineteenth and twentieth centuries. Consisting primarily of two major tribes (the Kikuyu and Masai), the region experienced negative colonial contact, pacification, exploitation, and land control, resulting in eventual independence under Kikuyu dominance and ongoing ethnic political tension. In this case, colonial ethnic manipulation and exploitation has aggravated intergroup strife on a long-term basis (Tigner 1976). Nigeria, originally a number of kingdoms also, experienced significant levels of outside European influence, indirect British rule, regional expansion and division, imposed federal arrangements, civil wars, tribal dominance, regional politics, and ongoing coups, wars, and military regimes. Again, unequal ethnic unity imposed by colonial outsiders causes endless strife and social problems for the society as a whole (Hatch 1970). Rwanda, referred to above, was originally invaded by the Tutsi tribe who conquered the Hutu and established a monarchy with the latter as serfs. Influenced by the Germans and then Belgians, the country became a trust under the latter, with an eventual Hutu uprising and achievement of independence. Subsequent political developments have included coups, military dominance, ethnic massacres, and mass refugee emigrations. Again, colonial manipulation of ethnic divisions results in inevitable intergroup violence (Newbury 1988). Both Burundi and Rwanda represent extreme cases of the disastrous effects of colonial ethnic manipulation. In this regard, Sri Lanka remains a battleground also: originally invaded by the Buddhist Sinhales and Hindu Tamils, the region was subject to Portuguese, Dutch, and then British rule with extensive tea, rubber, and coconut plantations. The country achieved republican status in 1972 and has been continuously subject to high levels of ethnic violence, reflecting a lack of minority rights protection and Tamil desire for independence. Once again, ethnic inequality exacerbated by colonial exploitation inevitably results in ongoing intergroup destructive violence (Wilson 1988). The Sudan also illustrates how forced regional ethnic unification may result in severe conflict: with the north predominantly Islamic and the south largely African, the country experienced Ottoman, Egyptian, and British dominance, eventually coming under Anglo-Egyptian control. Independence in 1953 brought political coups, regional conflict, riots against imposed Islamic law, increasing dominance of military councils, and rebellion against religious dominance. Again, colonial unification and manipulation create intergroup havoc (Holt 1961). Finally, Uganda represents an extreme case of colonial manipulation of ethnic diversity, particularly by the military, which, when combined with indirect rule, plantation exploitation, and protectorate status, resulted in long-term ethnic violence, a ruthless dictatorship, civilian massacres, and multiple army regimes. Three major ethnic groups subject to colonial division, manipulation, and army dominance, combined with economic exploitation have proved, once again, to be a highly volatile combination (Lwanga-Lunyiigo 1989). The above cases illustrate the manner in which colonial manipulation of ethnic groups through their unequal regional incorporation, economic exploitation, or differential political sponsorship, may create societal contexts which spawn dictators, civil wars, military elites, and long-term violence, sometimes in genocidal proportions. The generation and manipulation of ethnic pluralism in colonial contexts tends to have disastrous societal consequences.

Sometimes colonially-developed pluralism results in partition-ing arrangements, ensuring long-term, continuous intergroup vio-lence. This occurred in Bangladesh, Cyprus, India, and Pakistan. The first of these evolved out of eastern Pakistan, reflecting the country's Muslim interests, a group which had been subject to uni-fied British rule during the seventeenth century. Civil war fol-lowed its declared independence as Bangladesh and its politics re-main dominated by coups, military governments, and secessionist movements. Sectarianism has been this country's central ingredi-ent (Singh 1988). Cyprus continues to reflect divisions imposed by Greek and Turkish settlements and British control, formalized into a pluralistic ethnic state, long under Greek dominance (the coun-try's majority) and subject to continuous intergroup conflict, re-flecting both internal and external pluralistic interests (Joseph 1985). India, with its history of castes, dynasties, feudal states, Is-lamic influence, and increasing British control, either direct or in-direct, was divided into Muslim Pakistan, Hindu India, and later Muslim Bangladesh. Conflict over regional and ethnic issues has continued on a long-term basis, recently highlighted by the area's nuclear arms race with its neighbors. A very complex situation, this society remains potentially conflict-ridden, often in violent ways (Majumdar, Raychaudhuri, et al. 1967). Similarly, Pakistan, the arena of eighth century Muslim invasions, later unity with Northern India, and nineteenth century British rule, eventually es-tablished its independence, only to suffer coups, civil war, seces-sionism, and refugee influxes, reflecting its troublesome ethnic past and continuing sources of societal tension (Burki 1991). Again, these cases illustrate, in a particularly spectacular manner, the ex-tent to which imposed colonial unification, exploitation, and later partitioning aggravate intergroup conflict, making for long-term destructive violence, often on a regional basis. Particularly aggra-vating are the kinds of imposed inequities behind such discord.

Colonial societies may also produce high levels of mestizos, or racial mixtures, potentially increasing subsequent class conflict within them. Chile, Haiti, and Venezuela are relevant examples of this. The first of these saw extremely high levels of indigenous, working class, and Marxist conflict, resulting eventually in an ex-tremely repressive military dictatorship which only recently has started to give way to gradual reforms. Colonially-based class politics in a bureaucratic setting have typified this society (Kinsbruner 1973). Haiti, a French colony, was subject to plantation exploitation based on slavery, high numbers of mulattos, dictators including emperors and military elites, frequent outside intervention, attempted reforms, assassinations, and multiple military regimes (Dorinsville 1975). One of the poorest nations on earth, this country represents one of the most ravaged and conflict-ridden of all, representing one of the most negative examples of western colonialism. Finally, Venezuela was developed by African slave labor, rebelled against Spain, and has been subject to military control, civil war, reformist influences, and continuing attempted coups and economic problems. The population has a large number of mestizos within a clearly defined colonial class structure, representing a long-term, corrupt oligarchy. Such a setting has proved particularly destructive (Marsland & Marsland 1954). High levels of racial mixtures in colonial situations may exacerbate class-based and other forms of intergroup conflict within them.

The above cases illustrate the manner in which colonial elites may manipulate the minorities subject to their control in a variety of ways: unequal regional incorporation, abusive economic exploitation, differential political sponsorship, partitioning, and high levels of miscegenation are among the most evident. These arrangements tend to give rise to dictatorships, military elites, civil wars, class-based politics, and high levels of intergroup violence, occasionally genocidal in nature. In this manner, the external creation, manipulation, and exploitation of internal pluralism in the colonial context tends to produce very destructive levels of intergroup conflict. We turn to examine the nature and effects of colonial economic exploitation in more detail.

Colonial societies are typically founded on very high levels of external exploitation, often involving slavery or other forms of forced labor, and establishment of plantation economies. Consequent intergroup relations in these kinds of contexts tend to be highly negative and destructive. Such situations have occurred world-wide, including Africa, Central, North and South America, the Caribbean, Asia, and the Pacific, ranging from Angola to Zaire. The first of these was established by the Portuguese as a penal colony and used for the Brazilian slave trade and colonial exploitation, resulting in civil war, eventual independence, and con-

tinuing ethnic violence since that time. While espousing assimilation, the country's colonial elite was extremely racist in its treatment of the indigenous population (Henderson 1977). The Cameroon, affected by Portuguese explorers and German plantation
development, was subject to regional redistribution under separate British and French control, the latter of whom used forced
labor, later reunification, inclusion in a federation, and continuing
political strife in a less-than-democratic state (Le Vine 1971). Cape
Verde, controlled by the Portuguese, experienced slavery, a number of economic crises and other disasters, black revolts, elite
racism, low rates of social change, a one-party state, and economic
instability (Carreira 1982). The Comoros, long ruled by a Muslim
elite, experienced civil war, slave raids, increasing French control
and plantation exploitation, unity with Madagascar, eventual at-
tainment of self-government, continuing coups, and establishment
of one-party rule. The society remains traditional and largely rural
in settlement, reflecting continuing political volatility (Newitt
1984). Cuba also endured colonial domination, involving Spanish
conquest, colonization, plantation exploitation, slavery, increasing
outside influence, emergence of military dictators, and a communist revolution, with the society essentially under a state of U.S.
imposed siege. Its long-term history remains exploitive and repressive, regardless of what elite is in control (Suchlicki 1974).
Equatorial Guinea reveals similar experiences: Spanish colonialism and paternalism, plantation development, imported labor,
emergence of dictators and high levels of continuing political conflict. The society remains repressive and conflict-ridden, reflecting
its negative colonial past (Liniger-Goumaz 1988). Fiji, a small Pacific society, became a British crown colony with imported con-
tractual Indian labor for economic exploitation purposes, resulting
in eventual independence, with the Fijians controlling the land and
Indians dominating the political system, resulting in ongoing
racial tension and a recent coup. In this particular case; colonially-
produced ethnic pluralism has resulted in severe structural divisions with consequent intergroup problems (Norton 1977). Ghana,
founded on a number of Sudanic and Savannah kingdoms, became an African state subordinate to increasing British influence
and economic exploitation, subjecting the region to indirect rule,
increasing colonial control, the slave trade, and plantation devel-

opment. Independence was granted in 1957, after which the country has been subject to military and dictatorial rule. Its independence has remained unstable and problematic in a number of ways (Pellow & Chazan 1986). Grenada, another example, was discovered by the Spanish, exploited by the French using plantations and slavery, subject to eventual British control, the use of indentured labor, implementation of a new constitution, increasing political conflict, emergence of a dictator, as well as later revolution and U.S. intervention. The country remains poverty-stricken despite its developing middle class (Schoenhals & Melanson 1985). Guatemala is an even more violent plantation example: discovered by the Spanish, the area was subject to forced labor, racism, political extremism, economic exploitation, socialist movements, U.S. intervention, and continuous political violence. The country remains poor and conflict-ridden (Jonas 1991). Guyana, originally developed by the Dutch West India Company, was seized by the British, developed as a plantation economy with slavery and imported indentured Indian labor. Independence was achieved in 1966 with the country remaining under largely Indian political control, high levels of poverty, and socialist policies. Consequent racial conflict tends to be fairly high and ongoing (Despres 1967). Honduras, discovered by the Spanish, has also seen high levels of political extremism, external plantation exploitation, the rise of dictators, occasional political chaos, and limited reforms. Foreign economic interests have remained dominant in this country which lacks an indigenous elite and largely remains poverty-stricken (Morris 1984). Jamaica, famous for its sugar plantations, was explored by the Spanish, experienced exploitation of African slaves, many of whom rebelled, high levels of labor abuse and exploitation, immigrant Indian and Chinese labor, eventual emancipation and independence, with continuing economic problems and political instability. While majority suffrage was granted fairly early in its history (1944), the country remains politically volatile. (Black 1977). In a very different part of the world, Malaysia was subject to Hindu, Indian, Indian, Portuguese, and Dutch influence, with eventual British control, a plantation economy worked by Chinese and Indian labor, federation and secession, and continuing ethnic violence reflected in urban riots. Economic and political problems continue to plague the country (Andaya & Andaya 1982). Mozambique, a particularly negative case, was the scene of Arab and African trade, increasing Portuguese control and plantation development with forced labor, eventual battle for independence, and continuing ethnic civil war after this was granted (Torp 1989). The country has only recently experienced enough political stability to commence rebuilding its economy and has far to go to reach financial viability. Niger, earlier part of Saharan empires, came under increasing French influence, colonialism, and economic exploitation in the face of significant levels of ethnic resistance. Limited forms of autonomy began in the 1940's, with independence granted in 1960. Recent developments have included military coups and continuing political and economic problems. The country remains economically and politically problematic (Decalo 1989). Sao Tome and Principe, a group of islands off west Africa, were discovered by the Portuguese who exploited the area through plantations with abusive, forced labor. This was also a major center of the slave trade. Rising nationalism and political conflict resulted in their 1975 independence, dependent on high levels of foreign aid. The country continues to reflect severe legal, economic, and political limitations (Carreira 1982). Sierra Leone, a major slave trading area, was once dominated by the Portuguese also, but increasingly controlled by the British who established Freetown as an area for freed slaves. Under the latter's colonial control, the region became increasingly subject to a creole elite, underwent rebellions, and became independent in 1971. Subsequently, the country has experienced one-party government, riots, and emergence of a multi-party state. Recent conflict has included various disturbances and labor strikes (Crooks 1972). Singapore, once part of the Malayian Federation, was influenced by the Dutch and British, occupied by the Japanese, and colonized by the British, becoming part of its defense system in the area. Post-independence developments since 1959 have included federation with Malaya, later secession, an authoritarian government, and spectacular economic development (Drysdale 1984). South Africa, perhaps the world's worst example of extreme colonialism, was founded on Dutch-British competition for colonial dominance, racial and ethnic conflict, rising Afrikaner political control and English economic power, significant levels of black conflict, eventual independence, and continuing black violence (Dubow 1989).

Racial and ethnic pluralism in this hierarchical colonial society could hardly be more potentially conflict-ridden, despite its relatively peaceful transition to black majority rule. Suriname was also subject to Dutch and British influence, falling eventually under the former's colonial control. Economic exploitation included plantation slavery, the Dutch West India Company, immigrant Chinese and Indian contract labor, foreign mining interests, eventual autonomy and independence, with subsequent ethnic politics and continuing conflict, including a military coup and eventual civilian rule (Chin & Buddingh 1987). As indicated in the last chapter, the United States may also be viewed as a colonial society: subject to the domination and exploitation of a migrant elite, the country has endured racial slaughter, indigenous land expropriation, slavery, plantation exploitation, civil war, and continuing racial and ethnic violence particularly in the urban sphere (Goodman & Gatell 1972). While intergroup relations and conflict may vary somewhat by region and historical development, as illustrated in our previous analysis, the country as a whole continues to reflect its violent, colonial past in contemporary forms of inequality and interpersonal hostility. We turn finally to Zaire, the scene of long-term exploitation and intergroup violence. The region, originally an African kingdom, was explored by the Portuguese and British and subject to the slave trade. Eventually falling under Belgian dominance, the Congo Free State was exploited by King Leopold and colonial companies, abusively using forced labor for plantation development. Resistance emerged on a regional basis, resulting in its 1960 independence, consequent violence, rebellion and economic decline, and eventual repressive dictatorship. While recent political changes have occurred, the region remains highly problematic and conflict-ridden (Anstey 1966).

The above countries illustrate colonialism's most destructive features: external competition for colonial dominance, economic exploitation through plantation economies using slavery, forced labor, and imported (often indentured) ethnic workers, and imposed regional incorporation and/or federations aggravating internal pluralism, all of which tend to result in civil war, the rise of dictators and/or military elites, high levels of racism, political extremism, coups, as well as one-party and other forms of authoritarian government. In this manner colonial exploitation inevitably produces high levels of intergroup violence and related forms of political conflict. Particular kinds of elite may also arise in the colonial situation, a topic we turn to examine next.

Colonial societies, particularly those with immigrant majorities, may produce ruling elites on a class, bureaucratic, or oligarchical basis, resulting in the creation of problematic kinds of states, political activity and conflict. Both types of elites are to be found primarily in Spanish colonies, reflecting their feudal origins (Hartz 1964). Examples of class-based elites range from Argentina to Uruguay while oligarchies were formed in Brazil, Colombia, and El Salvador. In the first category, Argentina reveals a history of class conflict, dictators, military coups, Peronist populism, military control, civil repression, internal repression, external wars and, more recently, limited reforms and continuing economic problems. Military abuse of the civilian population has been particularly typical of its fairly recent history (McGann 1966). Bolivia, long part of the Inca Empire with an indigenous majority, has experienced aristocratic rule, high levels of elite-populist cultural conflict, high degrees of racial mixing, radical political movements, military rule, coups, temporary periods of democracy, and continuing political and economic instability. Its political history has involved extremism, high numbers of coups, military regimes, and continuing political volatility (Morales 1992). Ecuador, on the other hand, saw the decline of the Incas, increasing settler dominance and Indian labor exploitation, settler revolts, a civil war pitting monarchists against republicans, and increasing settler independence. Again, political instability has dominated its history (Hurtado 1980). Nicaragua, the scene of harsh Spanish colonialism and Indian decline also, saw the rise of urban and class differences, conflict between liberals and conservatives, increasing outside interference, the rise of a dictator, civil war, and continuing political instability (Walker 1981). Panama, a country located in a unique geographic location, was subject to outside federal arrangements and wars, U.S. involvement in the protection of the Canal, emergence of a Creole elite, use of African slaves and imported Chinese labor, liberal-conservative conflict, populism, long-term dictatorship, outside intervention, and continuing U.S. involvement. Essentially a U.S. protectorate, the country has a particularly violent history (Ropp 1982). Paraguay, while relatively egalitarian in its early colo-

nial development, has proceeded through disastrous wars, pop-
ulist revolts, dictators, high levels of mestizos, rise of a landown-
ing elite, and extended periods of military rule. Again, its political
history has been particularly volatile (Lewis 1982). Peru, like other
nations of the region, has also experienced high numbers of civil
wars, political instability, alternation between civilian and military
rule, limited reforms, rise of middle class elites, and recent insur-
gencies, reflecting continuing class-based inequality within the
country (Pike 1967). Finally, Uruguay also reveals liberal-conservative strife and related governments, limited reforms, large numbers of coups, periods of repressive military rule, and gradual democratization but with the re-emergence of authoritarian rule.
Again, colonial-based inequality is reflected in continuous political
instability (Gonzalez 1991). Clearly, in these societies colonial stratification results in high levels of political unrest, instability, alternation between left and right, emergence of dictators, frequent
military control, and re-appearance of authoritarian regimes representing elite interests of various kinds. Reflecting feudal-type
origins, perhaps, these class-based politics accomplish little for the
societies as a whole, particularly their indigenous and working
class majorities. Potential conflict is built into such societies given
their dominance by elite interests. These autocratic arrangements,
operating through dictators, military regimes, and others, are inherently conflict-ridden, occasionally resulting in genocidal, long-
term violence.

Some societies involved the creation of oligarchies or patrimonial states. Brazil is a major example of such a situation: based on
a landed aristocracy who successfully formed a patrimonial state,
they pursued their economic interests through the country's military control and development of a highly bureaucratic state. The
country's larger majority, including its labor and middle classes
and significant mulatto sector, lack power and status in a politically unstable environment (Keith & Edwards 1969). While this
case reveals higher levels of racial flexibility than others, and has
achieved a limited degree of recent political stability, Brazil has a
background of colonial elitism, exploitation, and long-term conflict. Its colonially-produced stratification structure is potentially
conflict-ridden. Colombia is particularly problematic: with a
legacy of Indian decline, black slavery, plantation economy, weak

state, and ruling oligarchy, the country has a continuing history of extreme political violence, despite recent state stability under an elitist government, aggravated by recent drug wars and guerilla incursions. The country is presently anarchistic in many ways, reflecting its violent past and present civil war conditions. The inequality produced by the past continues to haunt this tropical region (Bushnell 1993). El Salvador, a major coffee plantation oligarchy, was exploited by controlling urban elites who thrived on a largely export-driven economy, impoverishing the rest of the population. Dictatorships, military regimes, peasant rebellions, massacres, and coups inevitably followed, reflecting yet another violent autocratic setting (North 1985). Clearly, colonial exploitation in an oligarchical setting is particularly destructive for ensuing intergroup relations.

The above societies illustrate the manner in which colonial elites, particularly those who were feudal in origin, tend to produce conflict-ridden contexts. Countries ruled by autocracies, oligarchies, or patrimonial states tend to experience dictatorships, coups, military regimes, violent class conflict, political instability, and continuous intergroup strife, reflecting the destructive effects of their imposed interests. In this manner, the translation of feudal arrangements into colonial dominance creates inevitable conflict.

We turn finally to other forms of external exploitation. These include mineral expropriation, low economic development, imposed unity, the negative effects of annexation, withdrawal, and a case of reverse colonialism. In the first of these, Zimbabwe and Zambia, originally Southern and Northern Rhodesia, were founded partially through mineral concessions obtained from the indigenous population. The latter experienced Portuguese slave traders, British missionaries, Rhodes' extracted mineral concessions, British colony status with high numbers of white settlers, temporary federation with Southern Rhodesia and Nyasaland representing capitalist economic interests, indigenous resistance to this imposed arrangement favoring whites, independence in 1964, the rise of a strong president, economic decline, and eventual political reforms. This colonial society has undergone significant levels of economic instability and political conflict during its history and development (Mulford 1967). Zimbabwe was also influenced by slave traders, developed through mineral concessions, economic exploitation of the colony by the British South Africa Company, 1923 self-government, admission to the federation mentioned above, collapse of this arrangement, white declaration of independence in 1965 to avoid black rule, resultant civil war, and 1980 independence, with ongoing ethnic conflict and economic decline, particularly affecting the indigenous majority very severely (Mungazi 1992). While different demographically, these two colonies were founded on colonial mining interests, exposed to further settler economic exploitation, subject to external political manipulation, settler resistance to majority rule in the case of Zimbabwe, and high rates of racial and ethnic conflict.

Lack of economic development, on the other hand, may leave an independent colony economically underdeveloped and impoverished. This was particularly the situation in Guinea-Bissau on Africa's northwestern coast. Originally a number of kingdoms, the country experienced the slave trade, increasing Portuguese control, economic interests, and exploitation but with little investment in the society's general economy. Independence was achieved in 1974, after which a military coup occurred with limited political reforms taking place in the 1980's and 1990's (Lobban 1979). In general, this poverty-stricken, pluralistic country has experienced high rates of political violence and instability, reflecting its colonial creation and exploitation.

External regional manipulation of colonial situations, particularly involving imposed unity, annexation, and later withdrawal from a conflict-ridden area, tends to aggravate intergroup conflict. This is readily apparent in Algeria, the former Yugoslavia, and the Yemen. The first of these was the site of multiple invasions, including the Berbers, Romans, Phoenicians, Arabs, Spanish, Turks, and then French, eventually coming under the latter's colonial control. Resistance in the 1950's led finally to the country's 1962 independence, after which it has continued to experience very high levels of political violence, including assassinations, army coups, and the rising threat posed by Islamic fundamentalists. This setting has been particularly destructive recently (Ruedy 1992). The former Yugoslavia, as is well-known, is a particularly bloody part of the world. Based on Serbian settlements and subject to Ottoman domination, the country annexed Slovenia and Croatia after World War I, followed by a dictatorship, the devastation caused by World

War II, Tito's Stalinist-type rule, limited reforms, increasing ethnic violence, and the secessionist civil war and 'ethnic cleansing' battles of the 1990's. Recent events have highlighted continuing ethnic massacres and apparent ineffectiveness of the international community to put an end to them (Dragnich 1992). While limited international intervention has occurred, the world watches in horror as ethnic genocide continues to occur, particularly at the hands of the Serbs. Thirdly, the Yemeni kingdoms, once controlled by the Ottomans, subject to military rule and British control, experienced civil war in the 1960's after British withdrawal and, despite their 1990 merger, have continued to experience high levels of sectarian conflict since then. The country continues to reveal very low levels of national integration and high degrees of sectarian violence. Clearly, post-colonial unity may aggravate rather than pacify previously developed sources of societal conflict (Stookey 1978).

We turn finally to Liberia, a case of what might be termed "reverse colonialism." Founded by freed American blacks, the American Colonization Society was formed to repatriate them to Africa. With limited U.S. aid, these ex-slave settlers negotiated a land deal with the indigenous population, defeated any opposition, and declared their independence in 1847. This unusual colony was ruled by a mulatto elite who discriminated against local blacks and maintained their political dominance until 1980, when a military coup brought the country under martial law. Later coup attempts, ethnic wars, and massacres have taken a terrible toll on this pluralistic society ruled for so long by a black colonial elite originally enslaved by the United States (Liebenow 1987). This unusual case, along with those discussed above highlighting mineral expropriation, low economic development and regional manipulation, highlights the long-term destructive effects of external colonial exploitation of a country regardless of the migrating elite's national origins.

The above societies are outlined in Table 11.2 by contact type and conflict level. It appears evident that, on the one hand, *when indigenous resistance and political development, self-rule, significant levels of economic growth, emergence of middle-class elites, and high levels of miscegenation* occur in colonial contexts, *more democratic, less conflict-ridden intergroup relations* tend to follow. However, when these situations involve *the creation and manipulation of unequal types of*

Table 11.2   Societies Subject to Colonial Status by Country, Type of Contact, and Conflict Level

Countries	Type of Contact	Level of Conflict
Gambia, Guinea, Ivory Coast, Malta, New Zealand, Senegal, Tanzania	Colonies which experienced significant indigenous political development, self-rule, and levels of economic development	Low conflict
Djibouti, Gabon	Colonies which experienced high levels of economic development	Low conflict
Australia, Canada	Colonies controlled by middle class elites which became democracies	Low conflict
Dominica	Island colony with very high white/black racial mixing and low levels of political nationalism	Low conflict
Myanmar, Burundi, Central African Republic, Chad, Congo, Czechoslovakia	Colonies with externally imposed/manipulated types of pluralism, resulting in dictatorships, civil war, and violence	High conflict
Kenya, Nigeria, Rwanda, Sri Lanka, Sudan, Uganda	Colonial manipulation of ethnic groups through unequal regional incorporation or differential sponsorship, resulting in destructive political arrangements	High conflict
Bangladesh, Cyprus, Pakistan, India	Colonially-produced pluralism and partitioning arrangements	High conflict
Chile, Haiti, Venezuela	High levels of class-based, colonially-produced mestizos	High conflict
Angola, Cameroon, Cape Verde, Comoros, Cuba, Equatorial Guinea, Fiji, Ghana, Grenada, Guatemala, Guyana,	Colonial exploitation, often involving slavery or other forms of forced labor, used to exploit plantation economies	High conflict

(continues)

Table 11.2 *(continued)*

Countries	Type of Contact	Level of Conflict
Honduras, Jamaica, Malaysia, Mozambique, Niger, Sao Tome and Principe, Sierra Leone, Singapore, South Africa, Suriname, United States, Zaire		
Argentina, Bolivia, Ecuador, Nicaragua, Panama, Paraguay, Uruguay	Colonially-produced class-based, oligarchical or bureaucratic elites	High conflict
Brazil, Colombia, El Salvador	Colonially-produced oligarchies or patrimonial states	High conflict
Zambia, Zimbabwe	Colonial mineral exploitation	High conflict
Guinea-Bissau	High colonial exploitation with low economic development	High conflict
Algeria, Yugoslavia, Yemen	Colonial regional manipulation	High conflict
Liberia	Reverse colonialism	High conflict

pluralism, partitioning arrangements, high levels of mestizos, establishment of plantation economies exploited through slavery and other forms of forced labor, the rise of colonial class-based or oligarchical elites, and other damaging forms of external exploitation, they tend to result in the emergence of dictatorships, civil war, and continuing intergroup violence, sometimes genocidal in nature.

Conclusions

This part of our analysis has revealed that nations may be supported as adaptive autocracies and bureaucratic states by outside powers in a manner which produces political and economic stability. However, when protectorate status consists of economic exploitation through forced labor and slavery, regional manipulation, and support for problematic traditional elites, high levels of intergroup violence tend to follow. Secondly, when colonies include indigenous resistance and political development, self-rule, significant levels of economic growth, development of middle-class elites, and high levels of miscegenation, more democratic, less conflict-ridden intergroup relations tend to follow. However, when this type of context involves the creation and manipulation of unequal types of pluralism, partitioning, high levels of mestizos, plantation economies exploited through slavery and other types of slave labor, the rise of class-based or oligarchical elites, and other damaging forms of external exploitation, dictatorships, civil war, and genocidal violence tend to result. Again, what appears crucial is the degree to which external influences facilitate indigenous political development or exploit societies economically and manipulate them politically, aggravating sources of potential intergroup competition and violence.

We turn to draw some general conclusions regarding intergroup relations on a worldwide scale.

12

Intergroup Relations Worldwide: Conclusions

This part of our analysis has examined intergroup relations worldwide with respect to the kinds of contact situations behind the formation of particular societal contexts, and their ongoing dynamics, relating to consequent levels of intergroup violence. We focused on six types of societal context: (1) those located in isolated and remote areas, less accessible to outside domination; (2) traditional societies, originally ruled by monarchies or other type of dynasty; (3) countries subjected to external control and/or cession; (4) societies exposed to high levels of outside invasion; (5) regions which became protectorates; and, (6) contexts formed predominantly through external colonialism. We found that, except for the first situation, each type was related to both low and high levels of intergroup conflict. Bringing the results of our analysis together, we shall attempt to draw some conclusions regarding the general nature of intergroup relations worldwide. We begin by summarizing the above trends by type of societal context.

Our analysis has highlighted the following types of contact situations and intergroup consequences:

1. isolated or remote countries settled by external refugees, plantation developers, or unusual elites, and/or subject to outside trusts (e.g., the Bahamas, Iceland, Seychelles, Mauritius, Micronesia, Costa Rico), tend to experience significant levels of political development and democratization. Consequently, they reveal relatively low levels of intergroup violence. While this is not to assume these factors are directly

causal in some fashion, key features of this type of situation
involve their relative freedom of outside interference, internal homogeneity, and gradual, peaceful democratization. In
contrast to the rest of the cases we analyzed, this type does
not typically experience high levels of strife and continue to
live in relative harmony;

2. traditional societies ruled by monarchies, or other kinds of
    dynasty, may experience varying types of contact sequences:
    resistance, internal unity, and gradual democratization, pro-
    ducing lower levels of intergroup conflict (e.g., Norway,
    Sweden, Denmark, Portugal); or outside invasion, control,
    manipulation, and interference, resulting in high levels of
    intergroup violence (e.g., Egypt, Laos, Iran, Iraq, Ethiopia,
    China, Somalia, Ireland, Israel, Turkey). Clearly, the latter
    have been negatively affected by their contacts with out-
    siders, reducing their internal freedom, boundaries, and lev-
    els of equality in contrast to the former's increased unity and
    independence;

3. countries subject to direct external control experience com-
    paratively low levels of violence when their security and in-
    dependence are guaranteed by other powers or their inde-
    pendence is facilitated by them (e.g., Andorra, Luxembourg,
    Switzerland, Mongolia). However, outside manipulation and
    exploitation tend to aggravate potential violence through
    their advancement of negative political arrangements, partic-
    ularly dictatorships, unstable monarchies, or trusts (e.g., the
    Philippines, Malawi, Cambodia, Papua New Guinea). Based
    on these cases, it is clear that outside powers may either fa-
    cilitate or exploit the countries subject to their control, with
    very different consequences;

4. the effects of invasion differ also. While relatively isolated
    situations not subject to occupation, whose independence is
    encouraged and not subject to negotiation, tend to avoid
    high levels of intergroup violence (e.g., Tuvalu), societies
    formed through external incursion, control, imposed monar-
    chies or dictators, and/or subject to partitioning, invariably
    experience high levels of intergroup conflict, including rev-
    olutions and civil war (e.g., Bulgaria, Italy, Afghanistan, Jor-
    dan, Mexico, Lebanon, Vietnam). Again, external forces may

either support a country's internal independence or impede it through control, manipulation, and exploitation;

5. protectorate status may also have relatively positive or negative consequences for those subject to it. Traditional societies may be supported as adaptive autocracies and bureaucratic states by foreigners, resulting in temporary political and economic stability in the face of social change (e.g., Bahrain, Bhutan, Kuwait, Botswana, Lesotho, Swaziland). However, when such an arrangement involves economic exploitation through slavery and forced labor, regional manipulation, and support for destructive traditional elites, negative intergroup relations tend to follow, including high levels of violence (e.g., Madagascar, Togo, Benin, Mauritania, Nepal). The potentially unstable nature of the former cases should be emphasized also in light of their undemocratic features, preparing them poorly for future societal developments;

6. finally, colonial societies, while generally the most problematic, reveal varying patterns of intergroup relations also, depending on their formative contact experiences. When indigenous resistance and political development, self-rule, high economic growth, emergence of middle-class elites, and high levels of miscegenation occur in colonial societies, more democratic, less conflict-ridden intergroup relations tend to ensue (e.g., Gambia, Senegal, Gabon, Australia, Dominica). However, when these situations involve the creation and manipulation of discriminatory types of pluralism, partitioning arrangements, high levels of mestizos, exploitation of plantation economies through slavery and forced labor, the rise of class-based or oligarchical elites, and other damaging forms of external exploitation, they tend to result in the emergence of dictatorships, civil war, and potentially genocidal intergroup violence (e.g., Myanmar, Chad, Kenya, Bangladesh, Chile, Angola, Jamaica, South Africa, United States, Bolivia, Zimbabwe, Algeria, Liberia). Again the contextual distinction is clear: development of economic and political independence, on the one hand, versus control, differentiation, exploitation, economic deprivation, and continuing political struggle on the other.

Conclusions

The above trends are outlined in Table 12.1 which summarizes conflict levels by societal context and major types of contact sequence within them. Examining these trends as a whole, it is possible to draw some specific conclusions as follows:

1. intergroup contacts which facilitate indigenous political development, resistance, self-rule, independence, traditional elites, bureaucratic states, and peaceful colonization tend to result in relatively harmonious intergroup relations;
2. however, contact situations which create dictators, partition arrangements, civil war, imposed monarchies, revolutions, and/or involve the use of forced labor to exploit plantation economies, creating unequal types of pluralism, and/or result in the emergence of colonial elites tend to create societal contexts which are highly violent;
3. what stands out in these trends is that *contact* situations or sequences are *more important* than societal *contexts*. Low intergroup violence may occur *even* in colonial situations *if* the kind of intergroup contact occurs which facilitates independence and harmony; alternatively, when societies which are often peaceful are subject to destructive outside treatment, ensuing intergroup relations tend to be conflict-ridden;
4. secondly, particular *kinds of contact sequence* differentiate between *low and high conflict:* contact situations which facilitate indigenous political development, self-government, constitutional reform, democracy, and independence tend to result in intergroup harmony; on the other hand, external invasion, partitioning, interference, manipulation, occupation, exploitation, imposed elites, and other forms of differentiation tend to create dictatorships, revolutions, civil war, and generally high levels of intergroup violence at occasionally genocidal levels;
5. underlying this historical typology is the degree to which a society's level of *independence* is either *facilitated* or *repressed* by the historical contact sequences involved in their formation and development. Clearly, the higher their independence, the greater the likelihood of intergroup harmony; alternatively, conditions which repress indigenous autonomy

Table 12.1 Types of Contact Situations and Intergroup Relations Worldwide

	Conflict Level	
Societal Contexts	Low Conflict	High Conflict
Isolated/remote areas	Refugees → high indigenous political development/ democratization; Plantations → high indigenous political development/truces; Protectorate/trusts → self-government; Settler elites → economic/ demographic decline	
Monarchies/dynasties	External domination → resistance → self-rule; Colonization → self-rule; Internal unity → constitutional monarchy	Invasions → dictators → revolution; External control → partition/secession; Interference → unity → civil war
External control	External guarantees → democracy/neutrality/ constitutional monarchy; External support → joint control → independence	External control/ manipulation → conflict; External occupation/ mandate → conflict
External invasion	No occupation → high local independence	External domination → imposed monarchies → dictators; External claims → revolutions; External control → partitioning; External monarchies → middle-class politics/ revolutions
Protectorates	External facilitation of traditional elites/ autocracies/constitutional monarchies;	Forced labor/slavery used to exploit plantations → violence;

(continues)

Table 12.1 *(continued)*

Societal Contexts	Conflict Level	
	Low Conflict	High Conflict
Protectorates *(continued)*	External facilitation of bureaucratic states → political development	External manipulations/exploitation of traditional elites → violence
Colonies	Indigenous resistance → political development → self-rule;	Creation/manipulation of unequal types of pluralism;
	Development of middle-class elites → high independence;	Pluralism and partitioning; Exploit plantation economies;
	High levels of economic development → local political development;	Rise of colonial elites → class-based politics;
	Peaceful colonization	Other types of external exploitation and manipulation

inevitably lead to ongoing social tension and violence. Consequently, it is impossible to ignore the conclusion that *facilitation of a society's political, economic, and social independence, as well as that of its subgroups,* is vital to ensuring intergroup accord at every level of human existence: local, national, and international.

Having completed our investigation of intergroup relations on a worldwide basis, we turn next to attempt a synthesis of national and international levels of analysis.

PART FOUR

Conclusion

13

Towards a Synthesis

This monograph has focused on the importance of intergroup relations, their major types, the comparative perspective and its relevance to this topic, intergroup relations in the United States specifically, and how these phenomena operate generally worldwide. We have made the following major points:

1. continuing types of social conflict in various parts of the world, often genocidal in proportion, persist despite human economic and technological progress, as well as attempts by international organizations to intervene and provide a wide variety of economic, educational, and military aid. Furthermore, significant levels of violence, even in western democracies such as the United States, continue to be visible, highlighting the widespread existence of "cultures of violence." This trend underlines the need to understand major factors behind the emergence of intergroup conflict and violence in historical, national, and international context in order to maximize peaceful conflict-resolution and significantly reduce potential intergroup violence;

2. we indicated that societies may be viewed as types of social structures, or combinations of particular contact situations, in which certain types of intergroup relations, positive or negative, may be situationally triggered in ways which are often unpredictable. Consequently, understanding these social environments, their historical development, and ongoing dynamics, becomes vital to dealing effectively with intergroup conflict and its destructive impact on all involved;

3. thirdly, we stressed that intergroup relations involve the kind of social interaction which occurs at individual, group, institutional, and societal levels, using group-based categories or definitions of particular contact situations. These operate at the individual level as attitudes and social identities, are very much part of intergroup dynamics (particularly social movements), reflect any society's institutional arrangements (e.g., the social organization of inequality), its historical development, and the global arena in which international reactions to conflict take place. They also occur in particular economic contexts, ecological locations, and political situations, reflecting the differential effects of both internal and external factors on them. We highlighted the importance of their ecological, demographic, and economic environments in this attempt to take a multi-level approach to these complex phenomena;

4. we underscored that the comparative approach to this subject permits the analyst to develop an awareness of the major factors defining such dynamics at all levels of society within the processes of any nation's shift from the more traditional to the modern industrial type. This particular method, while complex logically and methodologically, affords the researcher possible explication of major factors underlying a continuum along which a number of cases may be examined. In the case of intergroup relations, this method provides the observer with insight into the kinds of societal contexts within which they have emerged and change over time;

5. focusing on comparative intergroup relations specifically, we delineated two major types of elite situations: indigenous and migrant rulers with respect to their varying historical, ecological, economic, sociocultural, political, psychological and consequent intergroup relations differences. We concluded that migrant elites tend to be small, exploitive, ethnocentric, manipulative, destructive, and discriminatory, resulting in negative intergroup dynamics. Indigenous rulers, on the other hand, are more likely to be larger, less competitive and manipulative, creating more harmonious societal settings and social relations;

6. we examined intergroup relations within the United States as reflecting its colonial foundation, elite values, institutionalized inequality, adverse historical frontiers, continuity of negative intergroup contact, hierarchical, elitist social structure, and conservative response to social change. We also placed intergroup relations at the state level along a colonial continuum, ranging from the least to highest types of colonialism, based on differential location, type of societal foundation (*viz.*, types of migration, subordination, importation, and use of slavery), and consequent intergroup relations (positive or negative). We examined isolated and less colonial situations, states initially controlled by adjacent powers, those dominated by invading whites, and the most colonial, typically involving slavery and highly negative race relations. We concluded that a society's relative access, formative intergroup sequences, and general dynamics are crucial to appreciating its internal social relations;

7. finally, we examined intergroup relations worldwide with respect to the kinds of contact situations behind the formation of particular societal contexts relating to general levels of intergroup conflict. We examined a wide range of societal contexts, including the isolated and remote, traditional societies, those subject to external control and/or cession, countries exposed to high levels of outside invasion, areas which became protectorates, and situations formed predominantly through external colonialism. We concluded that particular kinds of contact sequence (rather than type of societal context) differentiated between low and high intergroup conflict: contact situations which facilitate indigenous political development, self-government, constitutional reform, democracy, and independence tend to result in social harmony; on the other hand, external invasion, partitioning, interference, manipulation, occupation, exploitation, imposed elites, and other forms of differentiation tend to create dictatorships, revolutions, civil war, and generally high levels of intergroup violence involving genocide on occasion. Based on this, we concluded that the higher a society's level of independence, the greater the likelihood of intergroup harmony; alternatively, conditions which repress indigenous autonomy inevitably

result in societal tension and violence. Facilitation of a society's independence is consequently vital to ensuring its internal social harmony. What appears crucial to intergroup harmony is any group and society's freedom to meet its needs adequately in its *own* way, without outside domination, manipulation, or exploitation of any kind. The above analysis also appears to indicate that some kinds of historical, ecological, societal, and political conditions tend to favor group independence and relative intergroup harmony while others have the opposite effect.

Bringing the above key points together, it is possible to view *intergroup relations* as a *function* of three major factors: (1) the predominant *kind of intergroup contact* involved in a society or region's *historical formation;* (2) general *type of societal context* involved; and, (3) the *kind of consequent societal structure* which has emerged from this. Types of intergroup contact include the following: indigenous/migrant versus migrant/indigenous contact; positive versus negative intergroup contact; low versus high levels of external migration, subordination, and importation; and the external facilitation of indigenous independence versus high levels of external exploitation of indigenous resources and labor. Clearly, a society's contact formation may either be predominantly positive, low in colonialism and external exploitation, or largely negative, colonial, and exploitive in nature. Some formative experiences facilitate political development, democratization, self-government, and local independence while others encourage the rise of dictators, political division, civil war, revolutions, external exploitation, and the rise of colonial elites. The former tend to reinforce relative intergroup harmony; the latter often produce destructive societal violence. What is most relevant is the effect of such societal formations on internal levels of freedom, either facilitating or inhibiting independent need-fulfillment and consequent levels of intergroup harmony or violence. Consequently, conflict is more like to be triggered in some societal contexts, particularly the negative type, than others.

Societal settings include more isolated sites as well as the highly accessible, and situations varying from low to high colonialism, both within a society and worldwide. More remote situations and traditional monarchies or dynasties epitomize lower levels of colonialism, societies exposed to external control and invasion involve medium levels of external domination, with protectorates and colonies the highest. Some societies have remained isolated for extended periods of time (e.g., Iceland) or subject to *gradual*, peaceful domination (e.g., Hawaii), for example, in contrast to the highly accessible and heavily colonized.

Types of societal structure also vary in the nature of their elites, levels of pluralism, types of intergroup policies, and economic arrangements. Generally, elites may be large, less conservative, ethnocentric, and exploitive or small and high on these dimensions. Societies may also be lower in pluralism, degrees of segregation and discrimination, with more unified labor markets versus those more pluralistic, segregated, discriminatory, and economically segmented.

Finally, consequent intergroup relations tend to vary in levels of social conflict, independence, elitism, internal inequality, demographic and economic dynamics, and ongoing violence. Some tend to be more harmonious, independent, equalitarian, assimilationist and peaceful with others reflecting much higher levels of conflict, inequality, segregation and turbulence.

The above factors are outlined in Table 13.1, highlighting the interrelationship among formative contact type, societal contexts, types of society, and consequent intergroup relations.

Implicit in this analysis is the importance of certain kinds of historical contact, societal contexts, and types of society to positive or negative intergroup relations. Indigenous/migrant, positive, independent types of historical contact in situations largely lacking in colonialism, with large, tolerant, non-exploitive elites tend to be associated with lower levels of intergroup conflict and more stable ongoing societal situations. On the other hand, migrant/indigenous, negative, exploitive, colonial types of historical contact, with small, conservative, exploitive elites appear largely to result in higher levels of intergroup violence and unstable societal conditions. While it would be naive and simplistic to assume these contact types and their consequences are causally connected in any uniform manner, these general trends appear to be remarkably consistent within particular societies and others worldwide. What appears most crucial in any specific case are the *particular*

Table 13.1 Major Factors Behind Intergroup Relations

Type of Contact →	Societal Contexts →	Types of Society →	Types of Intergroup Relations
indigenous/migrant vs. migrant/indigenous contact;	isolated vs. highly accessible sites;	elites;	high vs. low independence;
positive vs. negative intergroup contact;	low vs. high internal colonialism;	large vs. very small;	low vs. high levels of intergroup conflict;
low vs. high external migration, subordination, importation;	types of colonial origin;	low vs. highly conservative;	indigenous vs. imposed social arrangements;
facilitation of indigenous independence or exploitation	low vs. high colonialism;	low vs. highly ethnocentric;	low vs. high minority unity and conflict;
	remote situations;	low vs. high exploitation;	low vs. high elite societal domination;
	traditional monarchies;	low vs. high slavery/forced labor;	positive vs. negative postcolonial consequences;
	societies subject to external control;	low vs. high pluralism;	high vs. low levels of indigenous groups;
	societies subject to external invasion;	low vs. high segregation and discrimination;	high vs. low minority economic assimilation;
	protectorates;	unified vs. segmented labor markets	controlled vs. uncontrolled immigration
	colonies		

conditions under which groups come into contact with one another, consequent *type of society formed,* and the *influence of these factors* on subsequent intergroup relations within this context. Again, however, it is important to emphasize that it is the dynamics of distinct types of intergroup contact rather than the kind of context involved with appears to account most for subsequent intergroup relations. Thus, some kinds of intergroup contact appear to reduce indigenous independence, increase inequality and exploitation, and aggravate societal violence while others accomplish the opposite. While problematic contacts are more like to occur in specific contexts (e.g., colonial exploitation), this is not *always* the case: outsiders, for example, may choose to facilitate indigenous independence even under colonial conditions, depending on the circumstances involved. The optimistic implications of this result involve the possibility of improving intergroup relations even under previously negative conditions by introducing positive intergroup contacts within them, despite the complexities involved. We turn to consider such policy matters in the next chapter.

14

Major Conclusions

In this concluding chapter, we shall attempt to delineate the study's major policy implications, discuss its relevance to contemporary social issues within the United States, and outline sociology's possible contributions to these questions in the approaching millennium.

Literature focusing on improving intergroup relations, whether racial, minority, or otherwise, has traditionally focused on the problem's particular *level of analysis:* individual, group, institutional, societal, and international. In earlier decades, for example, major emphasis was placed on the problem as attitudinal, requiring psychological analysis and treatment, particularly in the form of positive socialization in educational settings (Kinloch 1974). While reduction of negative stereotypes and consequent social distance is obviously desirable, there are clearly other more structural factors involved. Others began to emphasize the need for community development, organization, improved relations with the police, and formation of empowering social movements. While such an approach is clearly important, the larger power context in which such changes are effected needs to be recognized, particularly in the manner it reinforces internal inequality and adapts to attempted change in a manner which retains dominance. Recognizing the structural nature of racism or other forms of minority exploitation has also been underlined in institutional analyses of this issue (Feagin & Feagin 1978), stressing the need to increase minority access and their resources, removing damaging stereotypes in these organizational environments. Related to this was a major emphasis on de-segregation, particularly in education, involving busing and related policies favoring integration (Kinloch 1974; 1979). Crucial, according to these policies, was the need to remove the structural significance of minority inequality in any society's institutional arrangements at every level within it. Finally, at the societal level, analysts have argued for power balances in the context of international security, increasing relevance of conflict-management, general importance of political development, particularly democratization (Banks 1984), and continuing use of economic aid and military intervention in the worldwide arena, particularly the United Nations. Comparative perspectives on this subject, as we stressed earlier, have also focused on societal development and increasing relevance of a global or world economy. The main limitation of all the above policies is their unidimensionality: they tend to focus on *one* aspect of the problem *only*, overlooking their *interactive relationship* with other relevant factors, thereby failing to recognize the problem's continuation despite suggested changes. Attitudinal, community-based, institutional, societal, or international changes may *modify* rather than *significantly reduce* societal inequality and violence. Rather than facilitating minority freedom and independence, such changes may permit power elites to *adapt* to social movements and other changes in a manner which helps them *maintain* their dominance of the larger society or region, particularly in the context of conservative majorities. This is *not* to suggest such changes are unimportant; only to emphasize they may fall significantly short of actually *liberating* affected minorities, unwittingly contributing to continuing inequality and intergroup conflict.

This study has highlighted *one major conclusion: facilitation of a society's independence is vital to ensuring its internal accord.* In general, we found that the higher a society's general level of independence, the greater the likelihood of intergroup harmony; alternatively, conditions which repress indigenous autonomy and aggravate societal inequality inevitably result in societal tension and violence. This finding clearly emphasizes the need to promote freedom and independence at *every* level of a society: individual, group, institutional, national, and international. This also needs to be effected with respect to the *kinds of groups* which have been part of a each society's particular formation and ongoing relations. In this regard, ethnicity, race, and class require major attention. We turn to discuss specific policy recommendations relating to the United States specifically.

Social Policy in the United States

Looking specifically at the United States, it is obvious this society has barely begun to acknowledge the extent of general inequality within it, leaving aside the need to deal with this vital issue effectively. A number of specific policy needs emerge as follows:

1. the importance of highlighting and elaborating the application of *human rights* in this society, including those dealing with minorities, the death penalty, employment, and welfare. The society's "liberal democracy" myth continues to mask the resilient nature of inequality within it, abrogating minority needs and civil rights, particularly in the context of Protestant Ethic moralism;
2. the vital need to give maximum visibility to *peaceful methods for conflict-resolution* in a culture which is extremely violent and uses this in law enforcement, entertainment, and advertising. Significant steps to implement such an approach to social problems need to be taken at all levels of the society: individual, family, educational, law-and-order, political, and the media in particular. The nation's tradition of "frontier violence" has continued far too long;
3. the need to appreciate more fully the *state and local contexts* in which particular forms of inequality and intergroup violence have emerged, as discussed in chapter 5. This includes types and extent of colonialism, the historical and demographic conditions behind intergroup contact, and the kinds of structural arrangements which have emerged from them. Clearly, there are important regional variations in these environments and associated issues which need to be taken into account when addressing contemporary social problems within them. Applying national economic aid based on assumed state homogeneity is naive, simplistic, and problematic in effect, potentially reinforcing rather than solving the problem concerned;

4. the importance of more fully appreciating the *variety of minorities in this society*—racial, ethnic, and others—with respect to their varying historical backgrounds, state contexts, present demographic condition, and need for full political, economic, and *independence* within the context of this plural society in a manner which facilitates their equality rather than adjusting to their demands in a typically conservative manner. The national emphasis needs to be on independence rather than amelioration in an assimlationist fashion;;

5. the need to encourage and facilitate *positive types of intergroup contact* at all levels in the society. This would involve positive, cooperative, equalitarian, democratic intergroup situations, emphasizing common tasks, bonds, and rewards in an open, tolerant, multi-cultural atmosphere. Such a recommendation implies moving far beyond the kinds of limited, often negative, unbalanced types of integration policies attempted in the past. Again, facilitation of minority rights and independence is vital in such a task; and,

6. the key role the *federal government* might play as *an outside facilitator and guarantor* of such equality and independence for *all* major social groups in the society, whether defined as a 'minority' or not. As our international analysis indicated, third parties may be very effective agents of constructive social change, protecting and facilitating the rights and independence of the situations they influence; however, it is crucial they intervene in a manner which effects minority freedom and independence rather than facilitating majority conservative adaptation to protest.

The above suggestions highlight this country's need to implement a significantly more human rights-oriented, peaceful, contextual, equalitarian, cooperative, and facilitative approach to the variety of intergroup relations within it. While these suggestions may appear hopelessly utopian, they remain relevant to "breaking through" the myopic, limited, self-reinforcing, ethnocentric, and essentially conservative approaches of the past which remain trapped in the liberal-disillusionment-conservative cycle of public policy. We turn next to address intergroup relations on the international level.

International Policy

International relations, while reflecting limited progress in recent years, also reveal the extent to which limited, elitist, and highly ideological views tend to dominate, miring effective change in petty regional political wrangling. Based on our analysis presented in chapter 6, a number of policy needs appear as follows:

1. given the overriding influence of contact sequences over contexts, the potential for *constructive outside intervention* is clear, providing it is effected in a manner which facilitates group independence and harmony rather than external interests. While obviously a complex task, such mediation requires far greater attention and implementation in the international arena. Too often, such action appears late and ineffective in guaranteeing minority rights and independence;

2. again, *protecting and implementing human rights in all societies* worldwide requires far greater visibility and enforcement than in the past. While some countries and organizations reveal higher sensitivity to this need, the international community needs to make this an extremely important priority in their treatment of policy issues, despite national protestations that these are "internal affairs." The use of economic aid as both weapon and reward might be implemented on a far wider scale than those most threatening such as Iraq and nations supporting terrorism;

3. as in the U.S. case, higher *appreciation of the varying contexts* both within and among different societies is required to deal effectively with modern issues rather than taking a relatively uniform economic or military approach to all of them. Foreign policy often appears to be unilateral and/or simplistic in intention and effect;

4. far greater appreciation of the *world's number and variety of minorities* and other groups within it is required to deal effectively with political conflict in the context of ongoing social change. In this regard, both contextual and group variety awareness are required to accomplish this. Far too often, nations are identified and dealt with largely in terms of their

governing elites without adequate concern for the multiple minorities within them, again with limited and often unanticipated negative consequences;

5. outside intervention should be used to *facilitate positive types of intergroup contact in national settings*, rather than supporting one or more party to the detriment of others, thereby aggravating rather than relieving intergroup tension. Such an approach would need to be based on the kinds of detailed information and insight emphasized above, taking an informed, multilevel approach to effective social change; and,

6. international organizations need to move beyond peace-*keeping* and military *intervention*, to the fully-informed understanding and facilitation of group needs and independence in *all* societal contexts. This implies *shifting to peace-making*, based on these criteria, and their continuing maintenance and support. Temporary interventions appear to have few, if any, long-term consequences for the situations involved (cf. Bell and Freeman 1974).

Together, the above proposals underline the need for constructive, rights-oriented, context and group sensitive, independence-directed, and peace-making external intervention into national conflict on the international level. While very limited progress has been made in this direction, it is clear that these agencies have a long way to go in actually *implementing* peace on a worldwide scale. Clearly, a great deal more than mere intervention is required to bring about effective, harmony-creating social change. In what ways might sociology be helpful in such a complex task?

Sociology's Potential Role

Sociology, particularly in its professional form, has tended to involve attempts by establishment thinkers to impose scientific rationality on contemporary society in a manner which reflects their own ideological interests rather than modifying the social order effectively to deal with its social problems, particularly inequality (Kinloch 1981; 1994). Their models of societal types have been limited and ethnocentric, highlighting differences, for example, between the traditional and contemporary, developed and underdeveloped, central versus peripheral position in the world system, and modern versus post-modern. Given the destructive effects of intergroup inequality and violence nationally *and* worldwide, both the profession and discipline require significant modification and elaboration. Among the more crucial are the following:

1. the obvious need for *greater diversity in professional member-ship*. Long the domain of middle class, white, European males, sociology's motives, perspectives, and types of insight have remained extremely limited, highly reinforced by an extremely competitive professional environment. While limited increased heterogeneity with respect to nationality, ethnicity, race, and gender have occurred during recent decades, the profession has far to go to reflect the larger social world adequately—ideologically, culturally, theoretically, or methodologically;

2. *professional organizations*, national and international, would consequently be more *diverse, open, democratic, and less restrictive in activity,* including access to publication outlets, concerned more with effective societal *change* than academic *prestige;*

3. such increased diversity should involve *less ego-centric motives and professional aims.* Major focus on understanding the modern world in order to *change* it in ways which result in significantly lower levels of inequality and violence should be primary rather than one of its minor, so-called 'applied' priorities;

4. higher levels of diversity should also result in *greater theoretical and conceptual diversity,* reflecting the world's complexity and moving away from the simplistic, relatively homogenous typologies of the past. Fuller appreciation and application of the comparative approach to societal variation should also occur, both intra as well as inter-societally, resulting in much broader and more detailed insight into the foundation and changing contextual nature of contemporary social issues;

5. *research methods would be more heterogeneous* also, moving beyond the simplistic positivism of the past to a richer appreciation of the "societal variety," its need for far more diverse

understanding, and their implications for the twenty-first century; and,

6. both the profession and discipline would become more concerned with *changing modern society* to make it more *peaceful and equalitarian* than advancing the ideological interests of its practitioners. Models of and methods for implementing such a context require priority attention in the academic and professional world, if the discipline is to attain meaningful visibility and relevance in the next millennium.

The above recommendations reflect the need for a more diverse profession in membership, theoretical frameworks, and methodologies, concerned more with facilitating the emergence of a harmonious, equalitarian society than advancing self-interest. Again, such a model is highly utopian, idealistic, and perhaps even unrealistic; nevertheless, if sociology is to be a positive, facilitating force in the forthcoming millennium, it will have to change. Otherwise, it will continue to reflect rather than contribute significantly to the solution of modern social problems.

Final Comments

The project outlined in this monograph has highlighted one major theme: *the need to facilitate group freedom and independence in order to maximize intergroup harmony;* otherwise, destructive violence will continue with inevitably disastrous consequences for all concerned. Responding to this central idea, the policy recommendations outlined above underline the need to guarantee and promote human rights, facilitate minority group equality and independence, effect positive intergroup contact, engage in active peacemaking, and ensure a diverse, democratic, and socially-conscious academic community. *Dealing with modern inequality* should become a *major concern* at every level: local, national, and global. Our data also revealed the possibility of advancing group independence and freedom, even in typically negative types of societal contexts.

Based on the above conclusions, it appears reasonable to be "cautiously optimistic" regarding the *possibility* of effecting significant degrees of intergroup freedom, independence, equality and consequent harmony in situations previously viewed as highly problematic. Ironically, however, many current orientations are quite the reverse: the U.S. government is not only in a state of 'gridlock'—"virtual shutdown" would be a more accurate depiction, as its participants pursue their individual interests in blind ideological fashion, with little, if any concern for the national interest. Political action in the international sphere, furthermore, is likewise 'lame-duck,' adaptive, and largely ineffective in the face of tyranny and genocidal regimes. General public mentalities appear to reflect the maximum pursuit of self-interest, while the media provide little critical insight into the limitations of this deplorable state, motivated instead by the profits offered by sensationalism and their "share of the market." The academic community, reacting to a state of increased competition and accountability, continues to pursue its self-interest at all costs, with little concern for the needs of its 'clients,' both within and outside the educational context. As a result of all this, it is difficult to be optimistic regarding the *likelihood* of implementing meaningful social change when it comes to intergroup relations; nevertheless, it is important to consider the necessary ingredients to bring this about.

Effecting social change which will significantly advance intergroup equality and harmony appears to require at least three major ingredients: large-scale *recognition* of the problem; detailed *understanding* of its *complexity;* and action-oriented *policies* which will actually *advance* group-based *freedom, independence,* and consequent intergroup *peace.*

Appreciation of the urgency and seriousness of the problem has a long way to go to catch up with its reality: conflict tends to be localized and many simply do not want to "get involved" if they feel it is not "their fight." In reality, however, potential violence affects us all in our socialization, reactions to others, and everyday experiences. The problem is clearly not distant; rather, it is 'next-door' in one fashion or another, and impacts everyone, not just those directly involved. Awareness of its ubiquity, multi-level operation, and societal impact is crucial to making a meaningful start in its effective reduction.

We have tried to delineate the problem's complexity in this study of the contextual factors, both nationally and worldwide, behind the most destructive types of conflict. Clearly, there are no simple, uni-dimensional solutions; rather, a multi-variate approach to the issue needs to be taken, combined with an appreciation of the structural environments in which this process emerges and comes to dominate particular situations. This project has highlighted the need to facilitate a society's independence at all levels within it, despite the historical emergence of problematic contexts, to ensure social harmony within it. Simultaneously, we underlined to need to understand the particular elements operating in those situations if effective social amelioration is to occur.

Finally, the task requires action-oriented policies designed to maximize group independence and freedom throughout any particular society. Rather than offering 'aid' designed to mollify minority protests, limited types of controlled "participation in the political process," or elite-designed programs of 'community-action,' public policy needs to appreciate and fulfill the political, economic, and social needs of *all* its subgroups in a manner which enables their independence rather than masking their dependence on the power elite. These kinds of goals, no doubt, will appear idealistic, abstract, unrealistic, 'lofty,' and possibly offensive to some; nevertheless, "business as usual" simply implies that nothing in this highly colonial society and world will change significantly. Thousands of largely innocent civilians will continue to be maimed and massacred on a daily basis, with little relief. Hopefully, the new millennium will prove to be markedly more peaceful than the last, reflecting at least some of the changes recommended above.

Bibliography

Albury, P. 1975. *The Story of the Bahamas.* London: Macmillan.

Anastasoff, C. 1977. *The Bulgarians.* Hicksville: Exposition Press.

Andaya, B.W. & L.Y. 1982. *A History of Malaysia.* London: Macmillan.

Andersen, R.O.M. 1975. *From Yankee to American: Connecticut, 1865–1914.* Chester: Pequot Press.

Anstey, R. 1966. *King Leopold's Legacy.* London: Oxford University Press.

Antonson, J.M. & W.S. Hanable. 1984. *Alaska's Heritage.* Anchorage: Alaska Historical Society.

Armajani, Y. 1972. *Iran.* Englewood Cliffs: Prentice-Hall.

Armer, J.M. & R.M. Marsh, eds. 1982. *Comparative Sociological Research in the 1960s and 1970s.* Leiden: E.J. Brill.

Ashmore, H.S. *Arkansas: A Bicentennial History.* New York: Norton.

Aung, M.H. 1967. *A History of Burma.* New York: Columbia University Press.

Avery, M.W. *Government of Washington State.* Seattle: University of Washington Press.

Bagley, C. 1970. "Race Relations and Theories of Status Consistency." *Race* 11: 267–289.

———. 1972. "Racialism and Pluralism: A Dimensional Analysis of Forty-Eight Countries." *Race* 13:347–354.

Baker, D.G. 1974. "Dominance Patterns in Anglo Fragment Societies." *International Review Of Modern Sociology* 4:148–164.

———. 1975. "Race, Power and White Siege Cultures." *Social Dynamics* 1:143–157.

Banks, M. 1984. "The Evolution of International Relations Theory." In M. Banks, ed., *Conflict In World Society, A New Perspective On International Relations.* Pp. 3–21. Brighton: Wheatsheaf Books.

Banton, M. 1967. *Race Relations.* New York: Basic Books.

———. 1983. *Racial and Ethnic Competition.* Cambridge: Cambridge University Press.

Banuazizi, A. & M. Weiner. 1986. *The State, Religion, and Ethnic Politics.* Syracuse: Syracuse University Press.

Barbour, N. 1966. *Morocco.* New York: Walker & Co.

Bardill, J.E. & J.H. Cobbe. 1985. *Lesotho: Dilemmas of Dependence in Africa.* Boulder: Westview Press.

Barraclough, G. 1957. *The Origins of Modern Germany.* Oxford: Blackwell.

Barth, F., ed. 1969. *Ethnic Groups and Boundaries.* London: George Allen & Unwin.

Batua, B.T., K. Lobi, et al. 1985. *Kiribati, A Changing Atoll Culture.* Kiribati: Institute of Pacific Studies.

Bawden, C.R. 1968. *A Modern History of Mongolia.* New York: Praeger.

Beatty, B. & R.O. Beatty. 1976. *Nevada, Land of Discovery.* Reno: First National Bank of Nevada.

Beck, W.A. & D.A. Williams. 1972. *California: A History of the Golden State.* Garden City: Doubleday.

Beckles, H.M. 1989. *White Servitude and Black Slavery in Barbados, 1627–1715.* Knoxville: University of Tennessee Press.

Bell, H.M. 1934. *Bahamas: Isles of June.* New York: McBride & Co.

Bell, W. & W.E. Freeman, eds. 1974. *Ethnicity and Nation-Building: Comparative, International, and Historical Perspectives.* Beverly Hills: Sage Publications.

Bender, G.J. 1978. *Angola Under the Portuguese, The Myth and the Reality.* Berkeley: University of California Press.

Berchen, W. 1973. *Maine.* Boston: Houghton Mifflin.

Berry, B. 1978. *Race and Ethnic Relations.* Boston: Houghton Mifflin.

Billig, M. 1976. *Social Psychology and Intergroup Relations.* London: Academic Press.

Black, C.V. 1961. *History of Jamaica.* London: Collins.

Blauner, R. 1969. "Internal Colonialism and Ghetto Revolt." *Social Problems* 16:393–408.

Blegen, T.C. 1975. *Minnesota: A History of the State.* Minneapolis: University of Minnesota Press.

Blue, J.T. 1959. "Patterns of Racial Stratification: A Categoric Typology." *Phylon* 25:364–371.

Blumer, H. 1958. "Race Prejudice as a Sense of Group Position." *Pacific Sociological Review* 1: 3–7.

Bobango, G.J. 1979. *The Emergence of the Romanian National State.* New York: Columbia University Press.

Bode, C. 1978. *Maryland: A Bicentennial History.* New York; Norton.

Bolland, O.N. 1977. *The Formation of a Colonial Society, Belize from Conquest to Crown Colony.* Baltimore: Johns Hopkins University Press.

Bollen, K. 1983. "World System Position, Dependency, and Democracy: The Cross-National Evidence." *American Sociological Review* 48: 468–479.

Bonacich, E. 1973. "A Theory of Middleman Minorities." *American Sociological Review* 38: 583–594.

———— & J. Modell. 1980. *The Economic Basis of Ethnic Solidarity.* Berkeley: University of California Press.

Bonilla, E.S. 1968. "Two Models of Race Relations: The U.S. and Latin America." *Revista de Ciecias Sociales* 12:569–598.

Bonner, P. 1982. *Kings, Commoners and Concessionaires.* Cambridge: Cambridge University Press.

Bowman, L.W. 1991. *Mauritius, Democracy and Development in the Indian Ocean.* Boulder: Westview Press.

Brass, P., ed. 1985. *Ethnic Groups and the State.* Totawa: Barnes & Nobles Books.

Brebner, J.B. 1960. *Canada, A Modern History.* Ann Arbor: University of Michigan Press.

Bridges, R.D. & R.O. Davis. 1984. *Illinois: Its History and Legacy.* St. Louis: River City Publishers.

Brown, R.D. 1978. *Massachusetts: A Bicentennial History.* New York; Norton.

Bryant, A. 1954. *The Story of England, Makers of the Realm.* Cambridge: Houghton Mifflin.

Burki, S.J. 1991. *Historical Dictionary of Pakistan.* Metuchen: Scarecrow Press.

Burton, J. 1990. *Conflict: Resolution and Provention.* New York: St. Martin's Press.

Bushnell, D. 1993. *The Making of Modern Colombia, A Nation in Spite of Itself.* Berkeley: University of California Press.

Caiger, G. 1969. *The Australian Way of Life.* Freeport: Books for Libraries Press.

Carmichael, S.S. & C.V. Hamilton. 1967. *Black Power: The Politics of Liberation in America.* New York: Vintage Books.

Carreira, A. *The People of the Cape Verde Islands, Exploitation and Emigration.* London: Hurst & Co.

Casanova, P.G. 1970. *Democracy in Mexico.* Oxford: Oxford University Press.

Channing, S.A. 1977. *Kentucky: A Bicentennial History.* New York; Norton.

Chin, H.E. & H. Buddingh. 1987. *Surinam, Politics, Economics and Society.* London: Pinter.

Choucri, N. & R.C. North. 1975. *Nations in Conflict.* San Francisco: W.H. Freeman & Co.

Clements, F.A. 1980. *Oman, The Reborn Land.* London: Longman.

Cochran, T.C. 1978. *Pennsylvania: A Bicentennial History.* New York: Norton.

Coleman, K. 1978. *Georgia History In Outline.* Athens: University of Georgia Press.

Colvin, L.G. 1981. *Historical Dictionary of Senegal.* Metuchen: Scarecrow Press.

Coram, R. 1993. *Caribbean Time Bomb, The United States' Complicity in the Corruption of Antigua.* New York: Morrow.

Corlew, R.E. 1981. *Tennessee, A Short History.* Knoxville: University of Tennessee Press.

Cotterell, A. & D. Morgan. 1975. *China's Civilization.* New York: Prager.

Covell, M. 1987. *Madagascar, Politics, Economics and Society.* London: Pinter.

Cox, O.C. 1959. *Caste, Class, and Race: A Study in Social Dynamics.* New York: Monthly Review Press.

Crooks, J.J. 1972. *A History of The Colony of Sierra Leone Western Africa.* Northbrook: Metro Books.

Crystal, J. 1990. *Oil and Politics in the Gulf: Rulers and Merchants in Kuwait and Qatar.* Cambridge: Cambridge University Press.

Curkeet, A.A. 1993. *Togo, Portrait of a West African Francophone Republic in the 1980s.* Jefferson: McFarland & Co.

Davidson, B. 1989. *The Fortunate Isles, A Study in African Transformation.* London: Hutchinson.

Davidson, J.W. *Samoa Mo Samoa, The Emergence of the Independent State of Western Samoa.* Melbourne: Oxford University Press.

Davies, J.S. 1948. *From Charlemagne To Hitler, A Short Political History of Germany.* London: Cassell.

Davis, E.A. 1969. *Louisiana, The Pelican State.* Baton Rouge: Louisiana State University Press.

Dawkins, M.P. & G.C. Kinloch. 1975. "The Black Ghetto: A Model and Rural Application." *Research Reports in Social Science* Nov.:22–43.

Decalo, S. 1989. *Historical Dictionary of Niger.* Metuchen: Scarecrow Press.

Degler, C.N. 1971. *Neither Black Nor White, Slavery and Race Relations in Brazil and the United States.* New York: Macmillan.

Derman, L. 1973. *Serfs, Peasants, and Socialists, A Former Serf Village in the Republic of Guinea.* Berkeley: University of California Press.

Despres, L.A. 1967. *Cultural Pluralism and Nationalist Politics in British Guiana.* Chicago: Rand McNally.

Dicken, S.N. & E.F. Dicken. 1979. *The Making of Oregon: A Study in Historical Geography.* Portland: Oregon Historical Society.

Dobie, E. 1967. *Malta's Road to Independence.* Norman: University of Oklahoma Press.

Dorsinville, M.H. 1975. "Haiti and Its Institutions: From Colonial Times To 1957." In V. Rubin & R.P. Schaedel, eds., *The Haitian Potential, Research and Resources of Haiti.* Pp. 183–220. New York: Teachers College Press.

Douglas, N. & N. 1986. *Vanuatu.* Alstonville: Pacific Profiles.

Dragnich, A.N. 1992. *Serbs and Croats, The Struggle in Yugoslavia.* New York: Harcourt Brace Jovanovich.

Drysdale, J. 1984. *Singapore, Struggle for Success.* Sydney: George Allen & Unwin.

Dubow, S. 1989. *Racial Segregation and the Origins of Apartheid in South Africa, 1919–36.* London: Macmillan.

Eckstein, H. 1966. *Division and Cohesion in Democracy, A Study of Norway.* Princeton: Princeton University Press.

Edelman, M. & J. Kenen, eds. 1989. *The Costa Rica Reader.* New York: Grove Weidenfeld.

Einarsson, I. 1987. *Patterns of Societal Development in Iceland.* Stockholm: Almqvist & Wiksell.

Elstob, E. 1979. *Sweden, A Political and Cultural History.* London: Rowman & Littlefield.

Farley, R. 1984. *Blacks and Whites, Narrowing the Gap?* Cambridge: Harvard University Press.

Farr, W.E. & K.R. Toole. 1978. *Montana: Images of the Past.* Boulder: Pruett Publishing Co.

Faulk, O.B. 1970. *Arizona: A Short History.* Norman: University of Oklahoma Press.

Feagin, J.R. & C.B. Feagin. 1978. *Discrimination American Style: Institutional Racism and Sexism.* Englewood Cliffs: Prentice-Hall.

Fehrenbach, T.R. 1968. *Lone Star: A History of Texas and the Texans.* New York: Macmillan.

Fieldhouse, D.K. 1967. *The Colonial Empires, A Comparative Survey from the Eighteenth Century.* New York: Delacorte.

Fleming, T.J. 1977. *New Jersey: A Bicentennial History.* New York: Norton.

Floyd, B. 1979. *Jamaica, An Island Microcosm.* New York: St. Martin's Press.

Fluker, R., G.K. Goodman, et al. 1981. *The United States and Japan in the Western Pacific: Micronesia and Papua New Guinea.* Boulder: Westview Press.

Fraenkel, P. & R. Murray. 1985. *The Namibians.* London: Minority Rights Group Report No. 19.

Francis, E.K. 1976. *Interethnic Relations, An Essay in Social Theory.* New York: Elsevier.

Franda, M. 1982. *The Seychelles, Unquiet Islands.* Boulder: Westview Press.

Fraser, T.G. 1984. *Partition in Ireland, India and Pakistan.* London: Macmillan.

Frasheri, K. 1964. *The History of Albania, A Brief Survey.* Tirana.

Frazier, E.F. 1947. "Sociological Theory and Race Relations." *American Sociological Review* 12:265–271.

———. 1957. "Race Relations in World Perspective." *Sociology and Social Research* 41:331–335.

Gaeddert, G.R. 1974. *The Birth of Kansas*. Philadelphia: Porcupine Press.

Gailey, H.A. 1975. *Historical Dictionary of The Gambia*. Metuchen: Scarecrow Press.

Gardinier, D.E. 1994. *Historical Dictionary of Gabon*. Metuchen: Scarecrow Press.

Gaspar, D.B. 1985. *Bondmen and Rebels, A Study of Master-Slave Relations in Antigua*. Baltimore: Johns Hopkins University Press.

Gerteiny, A.G. 1967. *Mauritania*. New York: Prager.

Geschwender, J.A. 1968. "Explorations in the Theory of Social Movements and Revolutions," *Social Forces* 47:127–136.

Glick, C.E. 1955. "Social Roles and Types in Race Relations." In A.W. Lind, ed., *Race Relations in World Perspective*. Pp. 239–262. Honolulu: University of Hawaii Press.

Golding, M.J. 1973. *A Short History of Puerto Rico*. New York: New American Library.

Gonzalez, L.E. 1991. *Political Structures and Democracy in Uruguay*. Notre Dame: University of Notre Dame Press.

Goodman, P. & F.O. Gatell. 1972. *USA, An American Record*. New York: Holt, Rinehart & Winston.

Gossett, T.F. 1963. *Race: The History of an Idea in America*. Dallas: Southern Methodist University Press.

Goudsblom, J. 1967. *Dutch Society*. New York: Random House.

Gouldner, A.W. 1966. *Enter Plato*. New York: Harper & Row.

Grambs, J.D. 1973. *Understanding Intergroup Relations*. Washington, D.C.: Association of Classroom Teachers of the National Educational Association.

Greenfield, S.M. 1966. *English Rustics in Black Skin*. New Haven: College & University Press.

Griffin, J., H. Nelson, et al. 1979. *Papua New Guinea, A Political History*. Richmond: Heinemann Educational Australia.

Grimshaw, A. D. 1973. "Comparative Sociology: In What Ways Different From Other Sociologies?" In M. Armer & A.D. Grimshhaw, eds., *Comparative Social Research*. Pp. 3–48. New York: Wiley.

Gunn, P. 1971. *A Concise History of Italy*. New York: Viking Press.

Gurr, T.R. & B. Harff. 1994. *Ethnic Conflict in World Politics*. Boulder: Westview Press.

Gyi, M.M. 1983. *Burmese Political Values*. New York: Praeger.

Halecki, O. 1955. *A History of Poland*. London: Dent & Sons.

Hall, W., ed. 1979. *The Kentucky Book*. Louisville:

Halperin, M.H., D.J. Scheffer & P.L. Small. 1992. *Self-Determination In the New World Order*. Washington, D.C.: Carnegie Endowment for International Peace.

Hamilton, V.V.H. 1977. *Alabama: A Bicentennial History*. New York: Norton.

Hanh, T.T. 1967. *Vietnam, Lotus in a Sea of Fire.* New York: Hill & Wang.

Harris, G.L., M. Ani, et al. 1957. *Egypt.* New Haven: Human Relations Area Files Press.

————. 1958. *Jordan.* New Haven: Human Relations Area Files Press.

Hartz, L., ed. 1964. *The Founding of New Societies.* New York: Harcourt, Brace and World.

Hatch, J. 1970. *Nigeria, A History.* London: Secker & Warburg.

Hechter, M. 1975. *Internal Colonialism, The Celtic Fringe in British National Development, 1536–1966.* Berkeley: University of California Press.

————. 1987. *Principles of Group Solidarity.* Berkeley: University of California Press.

Helmreich, J.E. 1976. *Belgium and Europe, A Study in Small Power Diplomacy.* The Hague: Mouton.

Henderson, L.W. 1979. *Angola, Five Centuries of Conflict.* Ithaca: Cornell University Press.

Henry, P. 1985. *Peripheral Capitalism and Underdevelopment in Antigua.* New Brunswick: Transaction Books.

Hezel, F.X. *The First Taint of Civilization, A History of the Caroline and Marshall Islands in Pre-Colonial Days, 1521–1885.* Honolulu: University of Hawaii Press.

Hingley, R. 1972. *A Concise History of Russia.* New York: Viking Press.

Hitti, P.K. 1959. *Syria, A Short History.* London: Macmillan.

Hjalmarsson, J.R. 1993. *History of Iceland, From the Settlement to the Present Day.* Reykjavik: Iceland Review.

Hoare, J. & S. Pares. 1988. *Korea, An Introduction.* London: Kegan Paul International.

Hoffecker, C.E. 1977. *Delaware: A Bicentennial History.* New York: Norton.

Holt, P.M. 1961. *A Modern History of the Sudan.* London: Weidenfeld & Nicolson.

Horowitz, I.L. 1966. *Three Worlds of Development: The Theory and Practice of International Stratification.* New York: Oxford University Press.

Hout, M. 1986. "Opportunity and the Minority Middle Class: A Comparison of Blacks in the United States and Catholics in Northern Ireland." *American Sociological Review* 51:214–223.

Hudson, G.L. 1991. *Monaco.* Oxford: Clio Press.

Hurtado, O. 1980. *Political Power in Ecuador.* Albuquerque: University of New Mexico Press.

Jahoda, G. 1976. *Florida: A Bicentennial History.* New York; Norton.

James, D.R. 1988. "The Transformation of the Southern Racial State: Class and Race Determinants of Local-State Structures." *American Sociological Review* 53:191–208.

Jonas, S. 1991. *The Battle for Guatemala: Rebels, Death Squads, and U.S. Power.* Boulder: Westview Press.

Joseph, J.S. 1985. *Cyprus, Ethnic Conflict and International Concern.* New York: Peter Lang.

Joshi, B.L. & L.E. Rose. 1966. *Democratic Innovations in Nepal.* Berkeley: University of California Press.

Kalek, P. 1971. *Central African Republic, A Failure in De-Colonisation.* New York: Praeger.

Kammen, M.G. 1975. *Colonial New York: A History.* New York: Scribner.

Kane, J.N., J. Podell & S. Anzoven, eds. 1993. *Facts About The States.* New York: H.W. Wilson.

Kann, R.A. 1957. *The Habsburg Empire, Study in Integration and Disintegration.* New York: Praeger.

Keith, H.H. & S.F. Edwards, eds. 1969. *Conflict and Continuity in Brazilian Society.* Columbia: University of South Carolina Press.

Kennedy, M.D. 1963. *A History of Japan.* London: Weidenfeld & Nicolson.

Kennedy, P.W. 1971. "Race and American Expansion in Cuba and Puerto Rico, 1895–1905." *Journal of Black Studies* 1:306–316.

Kent, J. 1973. *The Soloman Islands.* Harrisburg: Stackpole Books.

Khalifa, A.M. 1979. *The United Arab Emirates: Unity and Fragmentation.* Boulder: Westview Press.

Khuri, F.I. 1980. *Tribe and State in Bahrain.* Chicago: University of Chicago Press.

Kinloch, G.C. 1972. "Social Types and Race Relations in the Colonial Setting: A Case Study of Rhodesia." *Phylon* 33:276–289.

———. 1973. "Race, Socio-economic Status and Social Distance in Hawaii." *Sociology and Social Research* 56: 156–167.

———. 1974. *The Dynamics of Race Relations, A Sociological Analysis.* New York: McGraw-Hill.

———. 1975. "Towards a General Colonial Theory of Race Relations." *Research Reports in Social Science* Nov.:11–21.

———. 1977. *Sociological Theory: Its Development and Major Paradigms.* New York: McGraw-Hill.

———. 1978. *Racial Conflict in Rhodesia: A Socio-Historical Study.* Washington, D.C.: University Press of America.

———. 1979. *The Sociology of Minority Group Relations.* Englewood Cliffs: Prentice-Hall.

———. 1981. *Ideology and Contemporary Sociological Theory.* Englewood Cliffs: Prentice-Hall.

———. 1990. "A Comparative Study of Relatively Open, Harmonious Societies." *International Journal of Group Tensions* 20:167–177.

———. 1993. "The Comparative Analysis of Intergroup Relations: An Exploration." *International Journal of Contemporary Sociology* 30: 173–184.

————. 1994. "Introduction: Vital Issues in American Minority Relations." *International Journal of Contemporary Sociology* 31: 165–167.

————. 1997. "Racial Attitudes in the Post-Colonial Situation: The Case of Zimbabwe." *Journal of Black Studies* 27:820–838.

Kinsbruner, J. 1973. *Chile: A Historical Interpretation.* New York: Harper & Row.

Klein, G. & M.J. Reban, eds. 1981. *The Politics of Ethnicity in Eastern Europe.* New York: Columbia University Press.

Kostiner, J. 1993. *The Making of Saudi Arabia, 1916–1936, From Chieftaincy to Monarchical State.* New York: Oxford University Press.

Kossuth, L. 1854. *Hungary and Its Revolutions.* London: Henry G. Bohn.

Kranz, W., ed. 1967. *The Principality of Liechtenstein.* Vaduz: Liechtenstein Government.

Kren, G.M. 1962. "Race and Ideology." *Phylon* 23:167–176.

Kuper, L. 1970. "Continuities and Discontinuities in Race Relations: Evolutionary or Revolutionary Change." *Cahiers d'Etudes Africaines* 10:361–383.

———— 1971. "Political Change in Plural Societies: Problems in Racial Pluralism." *International Social Science Journal* 23:594–607.

Kurtz, L.S. *Historical Dictionary of Tanzania.* Metuchen: Scarecrow Press.

Lacey, T. 1977. *Violence and Politics in Jamaica, 1960–70.* Totowa: Cass & Co.

Lander, E.M. & R.K. Ackerman, eds. *Perspectives in South Carolina History.* Columbia: University of South Carolina Press.

Larson, R.W. 1968. *New Mexico's Quest for Statehood, 1846–1912.* Albuquerque: University of New Mexico Press.

Law, K. 1988. *Saint Lucia.* New York: Chelsea House Publishers.

Lawson, F.H. 1989. *Bahrain, The Modernization of Autocracy.* Boulder: Westview Press.

Layng, A. 1983. *The Carib Reserve, Identity and Security in the West Indies.* Lanham: University Press of America.

Leff, C.S. 1988. *National Conflict in Czechoslovakia.* Princeton: Princeton University Press.

Legge, J.D. 1964. *Indonesia.* Englewood Cliffs: Prentice-Hall.

Lemarchand, R. 1970. *Rwanda and Burundi.* New York: Praeger.

Le Vine, V.T. 1971. *The Cameroon Federal Republic.* Ithaca: Cornell University Press.

Lewin-Epstein, N. & M Semyonov. 1993. *The Arab Minority in Israel's Economy.* Boulder: Westview Press.

Lewis, I.M. 1988. *A Modern History of Somalia, Nation and State in the Horn of Africa.* Boulder: Westview Press.

Lewis, P.H. 1982. *Socialism, Liberalism, and Dictatorship in Paraguay.* New York: Praeger.

Liebenow, J.G. 1987. *Liberia, The Quest for Democracy.* Bloomington: Indiana University Press.

Lieberson, S. 1961. "A Societal Theory of Race and Ethnic Relations." *American Sociological Review* 26:902–910.

Lijphart, A. 1984. *Democracies, Patterns of Majoritarian and Consensus Government in Twenty-One Countries.* New Haven: Yale University Press.

Lind, A.W. 1969. *Hawaii: The Last of the Magic Isles.* New York: Oxford University Press.

Liniger-Goumaz, M. 1988. *Small is Not Always Beautiful, The Story of Equatorial Guinea.* London: Hurst & Co.

Lobban, R. 1979. *Historical Dictionary of The Republics of Guinea-Bissau and Cape Verde.* Metuchen: Scarecrow Press.

Longrigg, S.H. 1925. *Four Centuries of Modern Iraq.* Oxford: Clarendon Press.

Lopes, C. 1987. *Guinea-Bissau, From Liberation Struggle to Independent Statehood.* Boulder: Westview Press.

Lower, J.A. 1966. *Canadian History At a Glance.* New York: Barnes & Noble.

Luard, E. 1990. *The Globalization of Politics, The Changed Focus on Political Action in the Modern World.* London: Macmillan.

Lwanga-Lunyiigo, S. 1989. "The Colonial Roots of Internal Conflict." In K. Rupesinghe, ed., *Conflict Resolution in Uganda.* Pp. 24–43. Athens: Ohio University Press.

MacRae, D.C. 1960. "Race and Sociology in History and Theory." In P. Mason, ed., *Man, Race, And Darwin.* London: Oxford University Press.

Majumdar, R.C., H.C. Raychaudhuri, et al. 1967. *An Advanced History of India.* London: Macmillan.

Maloney, C. 1980. *People of the Maldive Islands.* Bombay: Longman.

Mandazza, I., ed. 1986. *Zimbabwe: The Political Economy of Transition 1980–1986.* Dakar: Codesria.

Manning, P. 1982. *Slavery, Colonialism and Economic Growth in Dahomey, 1640–1960.* Cambridge: Cambridge University Press.

Marmullaku, R. 1975. *Albania and the Albanians.* London: Hurst & Co.

Marsland, W.D. & A.L. 1954. *Venezuela Through Its History.* New York: Crowell.

Mason, P. 1970. *Patterns of Dominance.* New York: Oxford University Press.

May, D.L. 1987. *Utah: A People's History.* Salt Lake City: University of Utah Press.

May, S. 1987. *Pilgrimage: A Journey Through Colorado's History and Culture.* Athens: Ohio University Press.

McDonald, G.C., D.W. Bernier, et al. 1971. *Area Handbook for People's Republic of the Congo (Congo Brazzaville).* Washington, D.C.: U.S. Government Printing Office.

McDowall, D. 1983. *Lebanon: A Conflict of Minorities.* London: Minority Rights Group, Report No. 61.

McFarland, D.M. 1978. *Historical Dictionary of Upper Volta (Haute Volta).* Metuchen: Scarecrow Press.

McGann, T.F. 1966. *Argentina, The Divided Land.* New York: Van Nostrand.

McGovern, B. 1988. *Western Samoa.* Sydney: South Pacific Trade Commission.

McLemore, R.A., ed. 1973. *A History of Mississippi.* Hattiesburg: University & College Press Of Mississippi.

McLemore, S.D. & H.D. Romo. 1998. *Racial and Ethnic Relations in America.* Boston: Allyn & Bacon.

McLoughlin, W.G. 1978. *Rhode Island: A Bicentennial History.* New York: Norton.

Mead, J. 1982. *Wyoming in Profile.* Boulder: Pruett Publishing Co.

Meintel, D. 1984. *Race, Culture, and Portuguese Colonialism in Cabo Verde.* Syracuse: Maxwell School of Citizenship & Public Affairs, Syracuse University.

Meyer, D.G. 1970. *The Heritage of Missouri, A History.* Hazelwood: State Publishing Co.

Meyer, J.W. & M.T. Hannan, eds. 1979. *National Development and the World System.* Chicago: University of Chicago Press.

Micaud, C.A. 1964. *Tunisia, The Politics of Modernization.* New York: Praeger.

Miller, K.E. 1968. *Government and Politics in Denmark.* Boston: Houghton Mifflin.

Montville, J.V., ed. 1990. *Conflict and Peacemaking in Multiethnic Societies.* Lexington: Lexington Books.

Moore, J.W. 1970. "Colonialism; The Case of Mexican Americans." *Social Problems* 17:463- 472.

Morales, W.Q. 1992. *Bolivia, Land of Struggle.* Boulder: Westview Press.

Morgan, H.W. & A.H. Morgan. 1977. *Oklahoma: A Bicentennial History.* New York: Norton.

Morris, J.A. 1984. *Honduras, Caudillo Politics and Military Rulers.* Boulder: Westview Press.

Morrisey, C.T. 1981. *Vermont: A Bicentennial History.* New York: Norton.

Mulford, D.C. 1967. *Zambia, The Politics of Independence, 1957–1964.* London: Oxford University Press.

Mundt, R.J. *Historical Dictionary of The Ivory Coast (Cote D'Ivoire).* Metuchen: Scarecrow Press.

Mungazi, D.A. 1992. *Colonial Policy and Conflict in Zimbabwe, A Study of Cultures in Collision, 1890–1979.* New York: Crane Russak.

Nagel, J. 1966. *American Indian Ethnic Renewal: Red Power and the Resurgence of Identity and Culture.* New York: Oxford University Press.

Nesbit, R.C. 1989. *Wisconsin: A History.* Madison: University of Wisconsin Press.

Nielsen, F. 1985. "Toward a Theory of Ethnic Solidarity in Modern Societies." *American Sociological Review* 50:133–149.

Newbury, C. 1988. *The Cohesion of Oppression, Clientship and Ethnicity in Rwanda, 1860- 1960.* New York: Columbia University Press.

Newcomer, J. 1984. *The Grand Duchy of Luxembourg.* Lanham: University Press of America.

Newitt, M. 1984. *The Comoro Islands, Struggle Against Dependency in the Indian Ocean.*Boulder: Westview Press.

Newton, G. 1978. *The Netherlands, An Historical and Cultural Survey, 1795–1977.* London: Westview Press.

Noel, S.L. 1968. "A Theory of the Origin of Ethnic Stratification." *Social Problems* 16: 157–172.

Nolan, P.D. 1983. "Status in the World System, Income Inequality, and Economic Growth." *American Journal of Sociology* 89:410–419.

North, L. 1985. *Bitter Grounds: Roots of Revolt in El Salvador.* Westport: Lawrence Hill.

Norton, R. 1977. *Race and Politics in Fiji.* New York: St. Martin's Press.

Nowak, S. 1989. "Comparative Studies and Social Theory." In M.L. Kohn, ed., *Cross-National Research in Sociology.* Pp.34–56. Newbury: Sage.

Oliver, D.L. 1951. *The Pacific Islands.* Garden City: Doubleday.

Olson, J.C. 1966. *History of Nebraska.* Lincoln: University of Nebraska Press.

Olzak, S. 1992. *The Dynamics of Ethnic Competition and Conflict.* Stanford: Stanford University Press.

———— & J. Nagel, eds. 1986. *Competitive Ethnic Relations.* New York: Academic Press.

Opello, W.C. 1991. *Portugal, From Monarchy to Pluralist Democracy.* Boulder: Westview Press.

O'Toole, T.E. 1978. *Historical Dictionary of Guinea.* Metuchen: Scarecrow Press.

Pachai, B. 1973. *Malawi, The History of the Nation.* London: Longman.

Paquin, L. 1983. *The Haitians, Class and Color Politics.* New York: L. Paquin.

Park, R.E. 1950. *Race and Culture.* Glencoe: Free Press.

Peckham, H.H. 1978. *Indiana: A Bicentennial History.* New York: Norton.

Pellow, D. & N. Chazan. 1986. *Ghana, Coping with Uncertainty.* Boulder: Westview.

Peterson, F.R. 1976. *Idaho: A Bicentennial History.* New York; Norton.

Pettigrew,T.F. 1958. "Personality and Sociocultural Factors in Intergroup Attitudes: A Cross- National Comparison." *Journal of Conflict Resolution* 2:29–42.

Pike, F.B. 1967. *The Modern History of Peru.* London: Weidenfeld & Nicolson.

Pinard, M. 1971. *The Rise of A Third Party, A Study in Crisis Politics.* Englewood Cliffs: Prentice-Hall.

Playfair, G. & C. FitzGibbon. 1954. *The Little Tour: Andorra, Monaco, Liechtenstein, & San Marino.* London: Cassell & Co.

Powell, W.S. 1977. *North Carolina: A Bicentennial History.* New York: Norton.

Price, M.P. 1956. *A History of Turkey, From Empire to Republic.* London: George Allen & Unwin.

Price, R. 1993. *A Concise History of France.* Cambridge: Cambridge University Press.

Rabie, M. 1994. *Conflict Resolution and Ethnicity.* Westport: Praeger.

Ragin, C.C. 1982. "Comparative Sociology and the Comparative Method." In J.M. Armer and R.M. Marsh, eds., *Comparative Sociological Research In The 1960s and 1970s.* Pp. 102–120. Leiden: E.J. Brill.

Reed, T.H. 1924. *Government and Politics of Belgium.* New York: World Book Co.

Renard, R.D. 1988. "Minorities in Burmese History." In K. De Silva, ed., *Ethnic Conflict in Buddhist Societies: Sri Lanka, Thailand, Burma.* Pp. 77–91. Boulder: Westview Press.

Rex, J. 1970. *Race Relations in Sociological Theory.* New York: Schocken Books.

Rice, O.K. 1985. *West Virginia: A History.* Lexington: University of Kentucky Press.

Richardson, B.C. 1983. *Caribbean Migrants, Environment and Human Survival on St. Kitts and Nevis.* Knxville: University of Tennessee Press.

Robinson, E.B. 1966. *History of North Dakota.* Lincoln: University of Nebraska Press.

Rodman, S. 1982. *A Short History of Mexico.* New York: Stein & Day.

Ropp, S.C. 1982. *Panamanian Politics, From Guarded Nation to National Guard.* New York: Praeger.

Rose, P.I. 1968. *The Subject is Race: Traditional Ideologies and the Teaching of Race Relations.* New York: Oxford University Press.

Roseboom, E.H. & F.P. Weisenburger. 1969. *A History of Ohio.* Columbus: Ohio Historical Society.

Rose, L.E. 1977. *The Politics of Bhutan.* Ithaca: Cornell University Press.

Rosett, R. 1992. *Brazil, Politics in a Patrimonial Society.* Westport: Praeger.

Ross, M.H. 1993. *The Culture of Conflict, Interpretations and Interests in Comparative Perspective.* New Haven: Yale University Press.

Rothchild, D. & N.Chazan, eds. 1988. *The Precarious Balance, State and Society in Africa.* Boulder: Westview Press.

Rubenson, S. 1976. *The Survival of Ethiopian Independence.* London: Heinemann.

Rubin, L.D. 1977. *Virginia: A Bicentennial History.* New York: Norton.

Rubin, V. & R.P. Schaedel, eds. 1975. *The Haitian Potential, Research and Resources of Haiti.* New York: Teachers College Press.

Rubinson, R. 1976. "The World Economy and the Distribution of Income Within States: A Cross-National Study." *American Sociological Review* 41: 638–659.

Ruedy, J. 1992. *Modern Algeria, The Origins and Development of a Nation.* Bloomington: Indiana University Press.

Rule, J.B. 1988. *Theories of Civil Violence.* Berkeley: University of California Press.

Runciman, W.G. 1989. *A Treatise on Social Theory, Volume II: Substantive Social Theory.* Cambridge: Cambridge University Press.

Rutherford, N., ed. 1966. *Friendly Islands, A History of Tonga.* Melbourne: Oxford University Press.

Ryan, S. 1990. *Ethnic Conflict and International Relations.* Aldershot: Dartmouth.

Ryan, S.D. 1972. *Race and Nationalism in Trinidad and Tobago; A Study of Decolonization in A Multiracial Society.* Toronto: University of Toronto Press.

Sabatier, E. 1977. *Astride the Equator, An Account of the Gilbert Islands.* Melbourne: Oxford University Press.

Sage, L.L. 1974. *A History of Iowa.* Ames: Iowa State University Press.

Salibi, K. 1988. *A House of Many Mansions, The History of Lebanon Reconsidered.* London: Tauris & Co.

Salins, P.D. 1997. *Assimilation, American Style.* New York: Basic Books.

Santer, R.A. 1977. *Michigan, Heart of the Great Lakes.* Dubuque: Kendall/Hunt Publishing Co.

Schell, H.S. 1975. *History of South Dakota.* Lincoln: University of Nebraska Press.

Schermerhorn, R.A. 1964. "Toward a General Theory of Minority Groups." *Phylon* 25:238- 246.

———. 1970. *Comparative Ethnic Relations: A Framework for Theory and Research.* New York: Random House.

Schmid, C.L. 1981. *Conflict and Consensus in Switzerland.* Berkeley: University of California Press.

Schoenhals, K.P. & R.A. Melanson. 1985. *Revolution and Intervention in Grenada.* Boulder: Westview Press.

Schwartz, R.N. *Peru: Country in Search of a Nation.* Los Angeles: Inter-American Publishing Co.

Shalom, S.R. 1981. *The United States and the Philippines, A Study of Neocolonialism.* Philadelphia: Institute for Study of Human Issues.

Shephard, C. 1971 (first published 1831). *An Historical Account of the Island of Saint Vincent.* London: Cass 7 Co.

Shibutani, T. & K.M. Kwan. 1965. *Ethnic Stratification*. New York; Macmillan.

Sih, P.K.T., ed. 1973. *Taiwan in Modern Times*. New York: St. John's University Press.

Sillery, A. 1974. *Botswana, A Short Political History*. London: Methuen & Co.

Sinclair, K. 1980. *A History of New Zealand*. London: Allen Lane.

Singh, D.S.R. 1984. *Brunei, 1839–1983*. Oxford: Oxford University Press.

Singh, J. 1988. *Dismemberment of Pakistan, 1971 Indo-Pak War*. New Delhi: Lancer International.

Singleton, F. 1989. *A Short History of Finland*. Cambridge: Cambridge University Press.

Smith, R.F. 1966. *Background to Revolution: The Development of Modern Cuba*. New York: Alfred A. Knopf.

Snyder, D. & E.L. Kick, 1979. "Structural Position in the World System and Economic Growth, 1955–1970: A Multiple-Network Analysis of Transnational Interactions." *American Journal Of Sociology* 84: 1096–1126.

Snyder, F.G. 1965. *One-Party Government in Mali: Transition Toward Control*. New Haven: Yale University Press.

Spilerman, S. 1970. "The Causes of Racial Disturbances: A Comparison of Alternative Explanations." *Am,erican Sociological Review* 35:627–650.

Squires, J.D. 1956. *The Granite State of the United States; A History of New Hampshire from 1623 to the Present*. New York: American Historical Co.

Stanner, W.E.H. 1971. "Introduction: Australia and Racialism." In W.E.H. Stanner, ed., *Racism: The Australian Experience*. Pp.7–14. New York: Taplinger Publishing Co.

Steinberg, D.J., C.A. Bain, et al. 1959. *Cambodia*. New Haven: Human Relations Area Files Press.

Stephan, W.G. & C.W. Stephan. 1996. *Intergroup Relations*. Boulder: Westview Press.

Stevens, F.S., ed. 1971. *Racism: The Australian Experience*. New York: Taplinger Publishing Co.

Stookey, R.W. 1978. *Yemen, The Politics of the Yemen Arab Republic*. Boulder: Westview Press.

Suchlicki, J. 1974. *Cuba, From Columbus to Castro*. New York: Scribner's Sons.

Suwannathat-Pian, K. 1988. *Thai-Malay Relations, Traditional Intra-regional Relations From the Seventeenth to the Early Twentieth Centuries*. Singapore: Oxford University Press.

Taylor, C.L. & D.A. Jodice. 1983. *World Handbook of Political and Social Indicators*. New Haven: Yale University Press.

Taylor, D.M. & D.J. McKirnan. 1984. "A Five-Stage Model of Intergroup Relations." *British Journal of Social Psychology* 23: 291–300.

Taylor, D.M. & F.M. Moghaddam. 1994. *Theories of Intergroup Relations: International Social Psychological Perspectives.* Westport: Praeger.

Thompson, V. & R. Adloff. 1968. *Djibouti and the Horn of Africa.* Stanford: Stanford University Press.

———. 1981. *Conflict in Chad.* Berkeley: Institute of International Studies, University of California.

Tignor, R.L. 1976. *The Colonial Transformation of Kenya, The Kamba, Kikuyu, and Maasai From 1900 to 1939.* Princeton: Princeton University Press.

Torp, J.E. 1989. *Mozambique.* London: Pinter Publishers.

Toye, H. 1968. *Laos, Buffer State or Battleground.* London: Oxford University Press.

Tree, R. 1972. *A History of Barbados.* New York: Random House.

van den Berghe, P.L. 1976. *Race and Racism: A Comparative Perspective.* New York: Wiley.

Vilar, P. 1967. *Spain: A Brief History.* Oxford: Pergamon Press.

Viviani, N. 1970. *Nauru, Phosphate and Political Progress.* Honolulu: University of Hawaii Press.

Volgyes, I. 1982. *Hungary, A Nation of Contradictions.* Boulder: Westview Press.

Walker, T.W. 1981. *Nicaragua, The Land of Sandino.* Boulder: Westview Press.

Wallerstein, I. 1974. *The Modern World System: Capitalist Agriculture and the Origins of the European World Economy in the Sixteenth Century.* New York: Academic Press.

———. 1979. *The Capitalist World Economy.* New York: Oxford University Press.

Weede, E. & J. Kummer, 1985. "Some Criticism of Recent Work on World System Status, Inequality, and Democracy." *International Journal of Comparative Sociology* XXVI: 135–148.

White, T.D.V. 1968. *Ireland.* New York: Walker & Walker.

Wiarda, H.J. & M.J. Kryzanek. 1982. *The Dominican Republic, A Caribbean Crucible.*Boulder: Westview Press.

Wilber, D.N., E.E. Bacon, et al. 1962. *Afghanistan.* New Haven: Human Relations Area Files Press.

Williams, R.M. 1947. *The Reduction of Intergroup Tensions: A Survey of Research on Problems Of Ethnic, Racial, and Religious Group Relations.* New York: Social Science Research Council.

Wilson, A.J. 1988. *The Break-Up of Sri Lanka, The Sinhalese-Tamil Conflict.* London: Hurst & Co.

Woodhouse, C.M. 1968. *A Short History of Modern Greece.* New York: Prager.

Wright, J. 1982. *Libya: A Modern History.* London: Croom Helm.

Wright, J.W. 1994. *The Universal Almanac 1995.* Kansas City: Andrews & McMeel.

Yetman, R. 1975. *Majority and Minority: The Dynamics of Racial and Ethnic Relations.* Boston: Allyn and Bacon.

Name Index

Subject Index